THE DISCERNING NARRATOR:
CONRAD, ARISTOTLE, AND MODERNITY

ALEXIA HANNIS

The Discerning Narrator: Conrad, Aristotle, and Modernity

UNIVERSITY OF TORONTO PRESS
Toronto Buffalo London

ISBN 978-1-4426-4907-1 (cloth)   ISBN 978-1-4426-1937-1 (EPUB)
ISBN 978-1-4426-1936-4 (PDF)

Library and Archives Canada Cataloguing in Publication

Title: The discerning narrator : Conrad, Aristotle, and
modernity / Alexia Hannis.
Names: Hannis, Alexia, author.
Description: Includes bibliographical references and index.
Identifiers: Canadiana (print) 20220213127 | Canadiana (ebook) 20220213178 |
ISBN 9781442649071 (cloth) | ISBN 9781442619371 (EPUB) |
ISBN 9781442619364 (PDF)
Subjects: LCSH: Conrad, Joseph, 1857–1924 – Criticism and interpretation. |
LCSH: Aristotle – Influence.
Classification: LCC PR6005.O4 Z7428 2023 | DDC 823/.912–dc23

We wish to acknowledge the land on which the University of Toronto
Press operates. This land is the traditional territory of the Wendat, the
Anishnaabeg, the Haudenosaunee, the Métis, and the Mississaugas of the
Credit First Nation.

University of Toronto Press acknowledges the financial support of the
Government of Canada, the Canada Council for the Arts, and the Ontario
Arts Council, an agency of the Government of Ontario, for its publishing
activities.

Canada Council   Conseil des Arts
for the Arts   du Canada

ONTARIO ARTS COUNCIL
CONSEIL DES ARTS DE L'ONTARIO
an Ontario government agency
un organisme du gouvernement de l'Ontario

Funded by the   Financé par le
Government   gouvernement
of Canada   du Canada

Canada

For Michael and James

Contents

Acknowledgments

Some time ago, when I was floundering a bit, Lorraine Clark suggested in a rather Conradian way that I read *Lord Jim*. I am deeply grateful to her for discerning precisely what I needed at that time; for wonderful years of mentorship and friendship; and for our ongoing, immensely clarifying conversations about literature and ideas that began in her exceptional undergraduate English courses at Trent University all those years ago. Professor Clark's brilliance and her commitment to genuine intellectual inquiry are inspiring. When I was in graduate school, the late John H. Stape introduced me to the Joseph Conrad Society (UK) and the Joseph Conrad Society of America (JCSA) where I met learned and hospitable Conradians, many of whom have knowingly or unknowingly informed my work on this book. The JCSA's Bruce Harkness Young Conrad Scholar Award gave me the confidence I needed to pursue reading Conrad with Aristotle. I am also indebted to the JCSA for the chance to present some fledgling ideas on practical wisdom in *Chance* at an annual meeting of the Modern Language Association whose travel grant helped to get me there. Debra Romanick Baldwin was encouraging about my work on Conrad and Aristotle at its inception and generously provided much-needed and invaluable guidance on how to clarify my interpretative framework. Keith Carabine's gentle inquiries about my progress prevented my work from stalling for too long. Beyond Conradian communities, I am grateful to the brilliant Don Kjelmyr for requesting "more Lingard," and for his knowledge of intellectual history, ancient philosophy, and Nietzsche. My esteemed thesis director Christopher Fynsk provided ongoing moral support when, in the earliest stages of re-writing my dissertation to turn it into a book, I suffered from the kind of self-doubt that is particular to writers. My first English professor and dear friend Geoffrey Eathorne's genuine interest in Conrad's life and works, and his promise to read this book, gave me the motivation I needed to simply get things done. My dear friend Patricia Harper's forthrightness and sense of humour periodically dispelled the fog of uncertainty. Ruth Gotthardt's wit and wisdom made me less anxious thus more productive. For her constancy in friendship, encouragement, and insights into academic research and writing, I thank wonderful Shakespeare scholar Amy Scott. At the University of Toronto Press, I am indebted to Richard Ratzlaff for taking interest in my proposal; Mark Thompson for his patience and professionalism; and the remarkably attentive anonymous readers who recognized the manuscript's potential and helped me to write at my best. Senior Project Manager Deborah Kopka, copyeditor Stacy Lavin, and the production and marketing specialists at UTP, especially Stephanie Mazza, made the final stages of this project a pleasure. Finally, this book is for Michael and James, whom I love and admire so much and to whom I joyfully owe everything.

THE DISCERNING NARRATOR

Introduction:
The Deeper Significance of Sailing Ships

And the sailing of any vessel afloat is an art whose fine form seems already receding from us on its way to the overshadowed Valley of Oblivion. The taking of a modern steamship about the world (though one would not minimize its responsibilities) has not the same quality of intimacy with nature, which, after all, is an indispensable condition to the building up of an art [...] Punctuality is its watchword. The incertitude which attends closely every artistic endeavour is absent from its regulated enterprise. It has no great moments of self-confidence, or moments not less great of doubt and heart-searching. It is an industry which, like other industries, has its romance, its honour, and its rewards, its bitter anxieties and its hours of ease. But such sea-going has not the artistic quality of a single-handed struggle with something much greater than yourself; it is not the laborious, absorbing practice of an art whose ultimate result remains on the knees of the gods. It is not an individual, temperamental achievement, but simply the skilled use of a captured force, merely another step forward upon the way of universal conquest.[1]

Art is fond of chance and chance of art.[2]

While his modernist counterparts would register the anxiety of uncertainty, Joseph Conrad was more concerned about its disappearance. He conveys this preoccupation in the above excerpt from his memoir *The Mirror of the Sea* (1906), where we find something of a guide to reading his novels. Conrad knew the hazards of writing nautical fiction, commenting to his friend Richard Curle that "the public mind fastens on externals, on mere facts, such for instance as ships and voyages, without paying attention to any deeper significance they may have."[3] Thus in the above passage Conrad attempts to loosen his readers' "public" fascination with the modern steamer as a technological "fact" so that

they might consider its "deeper significance." He achieves this aim by
thinking through the myriad differences between modern steamers and
sailing ships and their implications for the kind of life a sailor might
hope to lead. Whereas the modern steamer eliminates (as far as possible) nature's unpredictability through the "skilled use of a captured
force," the sailing ship relies on the sailor's particular talents and the
mutable conditions at sea. Whereas the steamship regulates risk and
the potential for human error, the sailing ship offers a full and joyous
engagement with the realities of nature and human nature. In short,
Conrad is not only contrasting two ways of being in the world: he is
appraising or judging them in relation to an end – that of a fulfilling,
happy, or flourishing human life.

Conrad's meditation on the shift from sail to steam may invite
Romantic, thus inherently modern, interpretations.[4] We might, for
example, point out that he juxtaposes an industrialized, rationalist
approach to nature against an emotional and instinctive experience of
nature's grandeur. We may also recognize natural supernaturalism in
the sailor's "struggle with something greater than" ourselves. Such
observations clear the way for a Nietzschean interpretation of Conrad's fiction.[5] However, reading Conrad means remaining attuned
to the many dimensions of his thought, including his critical outlook on modernity and his apparent belief in the possibility of a "private" mind that has the potential to question the *status quo*. His texts
invite a wide variety of interpretative frameworks and incorporate
a Shakespearean range of traditions, including those in tension with
Conrad's immediate historical and ideological contexts. For example,
his claim that "intimacy with nature [...] is an indispensable condition to the building up of an art" has more in common with classical
philosophy than modern thought. He conveys art not, as Nietzsche
would have it, as an Apollonian illusion hovering over the Dionysian
abyss, but instead suggests at least a partially "intelligible" reality
that an artist attempts to convey: the artist's "intimacy" with nature
forms the foundation of "any art." Ancient philosophy appears even
more directly and specifically in Conrad's assertion that "incertitude [...]
attends closely every artistic endeavor," an echo – whether intentional
or not – of Agathon's aphorism in Aristotle's *Nicomachean Ethics*: "art
is fond of chance and chance of art."[6] If art itself contains no guar-
antees, it also depends for its very existence on chance; otherwise
it would merely replicate what already exists in the outward-facing
immediacy of the collective "public mind." Moreover, art's representation of reality includes a fond disposition towards chance itself as
the very ground of action.[7]

As I've begun to suggest, the premise of this book is that Conrad's moderate outlook on "incertitude" or chance, risk, and accident in nature and human nature becomes especially visible when we read his works with Aristotle. I argue that an Aristotelian reading of Conrad's fiction suggests a new trajectory in Conrad's literary career from its inception: an increasing ability to use narrative perspective in an appeal to the reader's private mind, so that we can see human beings as both worthy of compassion given our shared vulnerability to "incertitude" or chance, and accountable to reason given our considerable capacity for action. This trajectory in Conrad's fiction will reveal an artistic vision that is inherently more hopeful than his general reputation has allowed. Instead of a nihilist, Conrad is a realist like the ancient tragic poets in whose works, as Terry Eagleton reminds us, "no wide-eyed trust in material progress could patch up Philoctetes's foot, no social engineering retrieve Phaedra from her doom."[8] Eagleton explains that the most "persuasive" tragic outlooks combine pessimism and hope, for "if you diminish the human spirit in the manner of the nihilist, you deprive men and women of the criteria by which they might take the measure of their unhappiness; and the consequence of this is that they risk viewing their wretchedness as inevitable rather than intolerable."[9] Nihilists see no intrinsic meaning or potential in our actions. They see the nature of reality – the source of the "criteria" to which Eagleton refers – as fundamentally and inevitably unintelligible. Conrad is sceptical and critical, especially when it comes to ideals such as material progress or social engineering, but he does not ultimately espouse a nihilistic vision of things, as Aristotle will help us recognize.[10]

Conrad's affinities with Aristotle are unsurprising given what we know of his education and the history of intellectual life in Poland. He describes himself as having been "steeped in classicism to the lips"[11] at his public school in Cracow,[12] and Zdzsław Najder, one of Conrad's most important biographers, explains that Conrad would have encountered Aristotle in the Polish curriculum. Remarking that Conrad's "concept of human nature" is essentially Greek, Najder claims that "the relevant passages from Aristotle's *Nicomachean Ethics* were no doubt discussed during the introductory course of philosophy Conrad took in Poland."[13] Perhaps even more significant and less commonly known, however, is the history of Aristotle's influence among learned Poles, beginning in the twelfth and thirteenth centuries and solidifying in 1500 when "Aristotle was declared as the basis of all teaching at all faculties in Cracow (including theology, law, and medicine)."[14] Although Aristotle's popularity among Polish intellectuals saw a sharp decline during the Enlightenment,[15] we know that most eighteenth-century Europeans were generally familiar with Aristotle's texts, especially the *Nicomachean Ethics* and the *Politics*; and it was during Conrad's lifetime in the following century that serious study of both works flourished. Translator and critic T.A. Sinclair goes so far as to claim that "it was not until the [nineteenth] century, and the publication in 1832 by the Prussian Academy of the great Berlin Corpus of his works that the study of Aristotle as a Greek author was really taken seriously."[16] Thus it is more than merely fanciful to imagine young Conrad employing his knowledge of Greek – a subject he would have studied with Latin, French, and German given his gymnasium education [17] – by poring over the *Ethics*, his attention most likely caught by the ancient philosopher's references to sailors and seafaring.[18] There is proof, after all, that Conrad was thinking of Aristotle while writing and revising his work. For example, Jeremy Hawthorn notes the narrator's invocation of the *Poetics* with the words "pity and terror" in *Under Western Eyes*: "a hard-to-decipher deletion on the TS [the Philadelphia Typescript] suggests that Conrad deleted the words 'as Aristotle has said.'"[19] While Aristotle most likely cannot be counted as one of the storied authors who inspired the young, imaginative Conrad to join the merchant marine, he can and should be counted among those interlocutors who played a central role in Conrad's writing life and his artistic vision.

In the 1970s Edward Said noted a lack of critical attention to Conrad's "intellectual context."[20] At that time the scope of this attention was expanding to include antiquity, with Eloise Knapp Hay's Aristotelian reading of Conrad's political novels and Avrom Fleishman's consideration of Conrad's "organicist" politics.[21] More recently, David Adams's *Colonial Odysseys: Empire and Epic in the Modernist Novel* explores how modernist writers such as Conrad make use of the *Odyssey* (and elements of the epic) to communicate ambivalence about imperialism and to complicate concepts of national identity and home.[22] In *Rethinking Post-colonialism: Colonialist Discourse in Modern Literature and the Legacy of Classical Writers* Amar Acheraïou widens postcolonial frameworks for interpreting Conrad (among other modern writers) to include ancient Greek and Roman imperialist ideologies.[23] Shifting our attention from politics to philosophy, Debra Romanick Baldwin's "Marlow, Socrates, and an Ancient Quarrel in *Chance*" takes up the relationship between philosophy and art in Conrad's fiction. Part of a larger project on what Romanick Baldwin calls "narrative solidarity," her article explores how in *Chance*, "Conrad importantly modifies his Marlovian Socrates from the familiar philosophical model in order to recast the search for truth on his own artistic terms."[24] Nic Panagopoulos makes an important contribution to this philosophical conversation in his excellent article,

"Conrad's Poetics: An Aristotelian Reading of *Heart of Darkness*," where he notices the hybridity of ancient and modern thought in Conrad.[25] Taken together, these different studies affirm the value of considering the ancient literary and philosophical dimensions of Conrad's *oeuvre*. My contribution to this wide-ranging discussion is that Aristotle illuminates Conrad's moderate voice and outlook on "incertitude" or chance, risk, and accident – our guide to compassionate yet rational appraisals of human character and conduct.

Chapter 1, "Conrad's Vision of Things," draws from Conrad's letters and essays to consider the uniqueness of his voice and outlook at the turn of the century. Aristotle will provide us with a context for making sense of Conrad's self-differentiation from modernity, especially his declared focus on "action [...] nothing but action."[26] This work with Conrad's non-fiction will prepare the way for the next four chapters where we will trace his literary critique of modernity and his increasing ability to position the narrator as a compassionate yet rational thus equitable guide to the reader's judgment. To that end, chapter 2, "*An Outcast of the Islands*: Tragedy, Pathos, and Conrad's Narrative Appeal," presents Conrad's second novel as a formative moment in his literary career. Aristotle's theory of tragedy sheds light on this early masterpiece (1896) as an effort to develop a sceptical voice and historicist outlook on the extreme condition of modern pathos that quasi-Nietzschean protagonist Peter Willems embodies in contrast with the classically tragic Captain Linga. Jeremy Hawthorn rightly argues that *An Outcast* deserves more critical attention than it has received – but one can read the novel, as I do here, as "an apprentice piece" without joining those who have "dismissed it."[27] Chapter 3, "Seeing Jim's Virtues in *Lord Jim: A Tale*," looks at how *Lord Jim* (1900) deepens and refines *An Outcast*'s ambitious project. Aristotle's theory of tragedy helps us see that the novel contrasts two settings – the modern steamer called the *Patna*, and the premodern community of Patusan – in a pattern that recalls *An Outcast*'s historicist framing, and Peter Willems's two crises between which the narrator and Lingard implicitly distinguish. In *Lord Jim*, however, Charlie Marlow – Conrad's character-narrator and avatar – combines the compassion and reason that we see in *An Outcast*'s Lingard and unnamed narrator respectively, guiding us to consider that Jim is higher and nobler than his critics allow. The novel once again distinguishes between modern and ancient spheres of action while conveying great admiration for classical heroism and a deep scepticism about its possibility in the modern world. Chapter 4, "The Discerning Narrator in *Falk: A Reminiscence*," shifts from tragedy to comedy with a reading of this underappreciated novella (1903). *Falk* distils and clarifies what we encounter *An Outcast* and *Lord Jim* – the emergence of a moderate, literary perspective on incertitude in response to the extremes of modernity. Using Aristotle's concept of discernment (*sūggnomē*) to put a name to compassionate yet rational judgment, I explore how the novella's unnamed narrator develops discernment by participating in the uncertain world of action. Chapter 5 returns to Marlow in Conrad's *Chance: A Tale in Two Parts* (1913). When considered from an Aristotelian point of view, this late-career work can help us think through the limits of rule-bound and consequentialist outlooks, including their effort to deny or eliminate chance, risk, and accident from human life. Through Marlow's sceptical embodiment of practical wisdom, the novel implicitly revitalizes Aristotelian ethics.

In the pages ahead, I consider what Aristotle can do to shed new light on what I have found to be a compellingly moderate outlook on human nature in Conrad's fiction. If it sometimes sounds as though I'm claiming that Conrad was himself Aristotelian, this is because I think there are real affinities between Conrad and Aristotle – affinities that justify or ground my interpretative approach. I readily admit that even if it were possible to locate the texts and translations that Conrad may have read in Polish, French, and/or English, to make such a discovery meaningful I would be faced with the impossible task of determining how Conrad himself interpreted Aristotle's texts. However, there is a reasonable response to this apparent problem: given that history presents patterns and trends in Aristotle's scholarly reception, it *is* possible to retain a general sense of how Aristotle's works were received and disseminated in Conrad's day. We know, for example, that in the eighteenth and nineteenth centuries the interrelated *Nicomachean Ethics, Politics, Rhetoric,* and *Poetics,* each of which dwell on the mutable world of human activities and concerns, were more popular than Aristotle's purely philosophical and scientific works, such as the *Physics* and *Metaphysics,* which addressed eternal truths rather than social and political life. During this period, many writers, mostly Protestant, "enlisted Aristotle in a battle against materialism and scepticism"[28] and worked to "reclaim" his work from the reduction of Aristotle's texts to "arid technicalities" for which Ciceronian and Neoplatonic traditions were responsible.[29] While it is of course impossible to know exactly how Conrad (or any individual reader, for that matter) would have understood the *Poetics,* we can assume that given Conrad's education and intellectual life at the turn of the century, he shared in a tendency to view Aristotle's work as having ethical, rather than merely technical, interest and value. On the whole, this period in Britain and

Europe is associated with a liberation from neoclassical interpretations of Aristotle – a "continual process by which attitudes towards the work were both re-orientated and opened up in ways that are still with us."[30] Thus it would be more than reasonable to assume that there are more similarities than differences between Conrad's perspective on Aristotle, and our own.

1

Conrad's Vision of Things

I am *modern*.[1]

Conrad's point of view was far from modern.[2]

Locating Conrad as a modern writer is an uncertain affair. Of his 67 years, 47 were spent in the nineteenth century; however, his career as a writer did not officially begin until 1895 with the publication of *Almayer's Folly*. When it comes to his fiction, the problem deepens because one of the most powerful and valuable aspects of Conrad's *oeuvre* is the unsettling of all established categories of thought.[3] Then again, the destabilization of conceptual frameworks is in itself paradoxically symptomatic of twentieth-century literary modernism. If all literature, as Derek Attridge has poignantly argued, "consistently exceeds the limits of rational accounting,"[4] it is in the modern novel where excess becomes essence, or essence is enacted as excess – and so it may be that in venturing to classify Conrad's works as modern, readers will encounter the excesses that are the essence of Conrad's fiction but also the excesses, the fluidity, of the term "modern." In other words, the reader who ventures to conclusively fit Conrad's fiction into the framework of modernity will meet with much textual resistance and so many qualifications that the process of classification might seem to devolve into futility.

Nevertheless, it is a good place to begin – the notion of Conrad as "modern" – not only because he declares himself so to his first publisher William Blackwood (a declaration that we will soon read in context), but also because he was writing at the turn of the century when many interesting things were happening to the English-language novel. Between often conflicting modernist projects there are familiar aesthetic and existential threads: a conscious seeking after newness; a deepening awareness of self and world as inter-determined, plural, and multifaceted; and a displacement of object by subject. The monosyllabic solidity of words such as *Truth, God, Time* and, perhaps most significantly, the epistemic solidity of the *I* could no longer be taken for granted after Nietzsche, Einstein, Darwin, and Freud. Such shattering yet liberating transformations in the West surfaced in the fiction writer's relationship to language and to notions of character, point of view, time, and narrative structure. As Brian Artese points out in his work on Conrad and testimony, "like the literary modernism it helped to inaugurate, Conrad's fiction frequently presents itself as the testimony of locatable human agents, as opposed to the omniscience whose narrative purportedly is not subject to the disputability that testimony implies."[5] In works by Virginia Woolf, James Joyce, and Elizabeth Bowen we see the novel revolutionized, its aesthetics vibrantly redefined by the loss – confluent with the death of God – of the stable, omniscient, Victorian and Edwardian narrator.[6] Conrad's fiction, too, seems to emerge from the nexus of privation or disappearance and narrative innovation: the deferral of closure, the undoing of oppositions, and the calling-into-question of settled ways of knowing and being in the world place Conrad in conversation with the modern novelists named above.[7]

And yet the nature of Conrad's relationship with literary modernism remains in question. In his seminal work on Conrad and English Romanticism, David Thorburn argues that of all the major twentieth-century modern novelists, both English and continental, Conrad is the most difficult to categorize. Thorburn writes, "one feels towards [Conrad's] work to some degree as his friends seem to have felt about his person: that he was uneasy not only in that place of exile whose language he appropriated and greatly honoured, but also in the time in which he lived."[8] Thorburn argues that this personal uneasiness may account for what he calls a "double appeal" in Conrad's work, between Romanticism (or Wordsworthianism) and modernism.[9] However, the continuities between Romantic and modern outlooks are too pronounced to fully satisfy the duplexity that Thorburn seeks to address. In his Author's Note (1920) to *The Shadow Line* (1917), for example, Conrad recalls Thomas Carlyle's natural supernaturalism, suggesting an alliance with the Wordsworthian tradition from which Carlyle himself draws. Conrad writes, "all my moral and intellectual being is penetrated by an invincible conviction that whatever falls under the dominion of our senses must be in nature, and [...] I am too firm in my consciousness of the marvelous to be ever fascinated by the mere supernatural."[10] But his attachment to "the intimate delicacies of our relation to the dead and to the living, in their countless multitudes"[11] also signals Conrad's twentieth-century modernity, as he anticipates the work of his younger contemporaries such as Woolf and Joyce who continued in this still-revolutionary, if increasingly secular, emphasis on wonder in ordinary, everyday life. Underlying Romanticism and Modernism is a shared philosophical disposition, as Daphna Erdinast-Vulcan has observed: "Whether concerned with the question of origin or destination, Modernism has come to be identified with an ontology of ungroundedness, an intensely self-reflexive Romantic sensibility, which probes the boundary lines between subject and object, consciousness and world, self and text."[12] In this reading, a characteristically modern outlook refuses the notion of an intelligible human nature – or nature itself – from which to rationally deliberate about how to be in the world, in part because we are ourselves understood to be always already mediated by – that is, inscribed in – the very world that we might claim as the ground for such deliberations. There is, in this view, no way to disentangle ourselves from what we seek to observe and think through – and so we must consider all habits, practices, and insights into right action as constructs of infinitely debatable value. And so, given that modernity's "ontology of ungroundedness" extends and deepens Romantic subjectivity, if we seek textual evidence of Conrad's uneasiness (as Thorburn suggests) "in the time in which he lived," we must look to traditions, ideas, or aspects of his work that are very different from, if not simply incommensurable with, modern sensibilities and outlooks.

This book proposes that one of the most profound and illuminating tensions in Conrad's *oeuvre* is between his historical position as a modern writer at the turn of the twentieth century, and what his friend Bertrand Russell noted of Conrad's "adherence to the older tradition, that discipline should come from within":

> Conrad's view was far from modern. In the modern world there are two philosophies: the one, which stems from Rousseau, and sweeps aside all discipline as unnecessary; the other, which finds its fullest expression in totalitarianism, which thinks of discipline as essentially imposed from without. Conrad adhered to the older tradition, that discipline should come from within. He despised indiscipline, and hated discipline that was merely external.[13]

Russell observes that in Conrad's view, our actions should not be governed by "external" rules but should instead arise from intrinsic human qualities and capacities. Conrad's view, in other words, is moderate – falling between Rousseauvian and totalitarian extremes.[14] Zdzisław Najder provides a clarifying gloss on Russell's observation: "The 'older tradition' voiced here goes far back to ancient Greece," specifically "to Aristotle's dictum that man outside society is either god or beast."[15] Najder is alluding to Aristotle's *Poetics* which teaches that tragic figures are human because they are by nature both admirable (capable of excellence) yet flawed (subject to error and circumstances beyond their control). Our uniquely human nature is such that we live between the abstractions of god-like control and certainty on the one hand, and utter subjection on the other. The former articulates something of an excessive investment in the powers of rational intention (to the extent that this investment becomes irrational), and the latter speaks to extreme irrationality and unintelligibility. For Aristotle, as for Conrad, the richly complex position between these excesses where we perceive, deliberate, and "move" in our various spheres of action is what makes us human. If "discipline" comes from "without" – if it is approached "externally"– then we are hubristically attempting to eliminate uncertainty from reality, while simultaneously reducing human beings to passive "beasts" by robbing them of agency. Conrad's outlook – his "vision of things"[16] – includes a critique of modernity as characterized by extremes, including (again) the seemingly self-evident "ontology of ungroundedness" that informs those extremes.

Before turning to Conrad's fiction, we will look at select excerpts from five seminal letters, supported by key passages from the Preface to *The N[*****] of the "Narcissus"* (1897) and *A Personal Record* (1908), to consider Conrad's outlook on modernity and how he self-differentiates from what he observes in his modern contemporaries. Conrad certainly values innovation, showing a characteristically modern preoccupation with the new – but he is cautious about certain modern sensibilities and perspectives, and resistant to what he implies is a tendency to assume that the modern (or the contemporary) is the best, most authoritative or definitive point of view. Putting classical elements of character and action at the centre of his defence of literature, Conrad conveys an admirably impassioned yet measured voice and outlook that appeals to the same potential in his audience. In other words, Conrad's letters and essays will get us thinking about how a narrator might guide a reader (or listener) to see – without imposing an all-knowing voice on the one hand, and without retreating into the passivity of what Conrad refers to as "endless analysis" on the other.

On Being Modern

Eight large volumes of Conrad's letters are a testament to the importance of this mode of communication to Conrad's life and art. Readers can learn much from them about Conrad's ambivalence regarding modernism and his identity as a modern novelist. The excerpts below are from letters written under particularly difficult circumstances – although financial, professional, and domestic stress appears not to dampen but to inspire Conrad's capacity for eloquence and insight. Consider, for example, a letter he wrote on 31 May 1902 to his publisher William Blackwood. At this time, Conrad is struggling to finish "The End of the Tether" – a story that has been causing him trouble over some spring months of writing, in part because a portion of the manuscript was accidentally destroyed in a fire caused by an overturned lamp. Moreover, Blackwood, one of Conrad's greatest supporters, has just denied Conrad an advance, explaining that the company can no longer afford such arrangements. Further complicating the situation is the fact that Conrad has already begun what would become a twenty-year association with literary agent James Brand Pinker.[17] Under these various pressures Conrad composes one of his fiercest and most cogent declarations about his identity as a modern writer. He writes,

> I am *modern,* and I would rather recall Wagner the musician and Rodin the sculptor who both had to starve a little in their day – and Whistler the painter who made Ruskin the critic foam at the mouth with scorn and indignation. They too have arrived. They too had to suffer for being "new." [...] My work shall not be an utter failure because it has the solid basis of a definite intention: – first: and next because it is not an endless analysis of affected sentiments but in its essence it is action (strange as this affirmation may sound at the present time) nothing but action – action observed, felt and interpreted with an absolute truth to my sensations (which are the basis of art and literature) – action of human beings that will bleed to prick, and are moving in a visible world. That is my creed.[18]

Here we witness Conrad re-contextualizing his work, placing it in a wider, historical frame – so that his reader might shift his focus from proximal, pragmatic problems of creative and financial unrest and onto the creative conditions and reception of truly great works of art. Conrad argues that his fiction, like any form of art, is bound to suffer a temporary lack of popular recognition; he casts himself as a representative of literature among the great figures of the three other major forms of art of his time: music, sculpture, and painting.[19] An initially unfavourable reception should be read as a sign not of artistic failure but of success, for all great works are conditioned by their newness, and what is new and unfamiliar is – as history shows – at first rejected. And Conrad argues that he has an artistic vision: he shares in Rodin and Whistler's preoccupation with real, rather than mythical or ideal, life; he wants to represent "human beings that will bleed to prick."[20] Where Blackwood may see problems, he should recognize excellence.

Conrad clearly recognizes the persuasive force of the declaration "I am *modern*" for his reader. However, he also embeds in his address to Blackwood acts of self-differentiation from ideas associated with modernism. He sounds characteristically modern when he claims that the only "absolute truth" in art and literature is that of one's own "sensations." His description recalls the Romantic symbol of artistic creation – the Aeolian harp, with its passive reception of the winds of inspiration and its active production of music according to the structure and tension of the strings. Truth is not the stable referent towards which literary language aesthetically gestures; rather, truth is inseparable from the very process of literary creation itself. The absolute truth is that there *is* no absolute truth, and what remains is the individual artist-subject's effort to be as faithful as possible to what is only transitorily known and experienced through the senses. Still, the letter is nuanced and layered – complicating what may at first glance appear to articulate familiar, modernist ideas. The first clue is Conrad's use of quotation marks around the word "new" – reflecting his scepticism about novelty in art – suggesting at once that it is a superficial measure of artistic value or simply impossible.[21] This sceptical distance from the "new" is also reflected in Conrad's emphatic – almost defiant – reference to "action" and his "solid basis of a definite intention," an unwavering sense of purpose.[22] However, if we are to begin to recognize the significance of Conrad's phrase "nothing but action," and his parenthetical suggestion that an "affirmation" of action might seem "strange [...] at the present time," we must revisit the letter to Blackwood considering two other, seminal letters where Conrad explores his relation to modernity.

First, consider an early-career letter to Edward Garnett, Conrad's supportive reader and friend. Once again, Conrad is under much pressure. Three weeks earlier, T. Fisher Unwin published Conrad's second novel, *An Outcast of the Islands* – and Conrad is facing the uncertainty of life between projects. He has just set aside his manuscript of *The Sisters* (published posthumously, in 1928) to work on what would become the long-delayed novel entitled *The Rescue, A Romance of the Shallows* (1920). Also, he is about to marry or has just married Jessie George before the couple would travel to Brittany for five months.[23] Under such fraught conditions Conrad writes to Garnett of

the fidelity to passing emotions which is perhaps a nearer approach to truth than any other philosophy of life. And why not? If we are "ever becoming – never being" then I would be a fool if I tried to become this thing rather than that; for I know well that I will never be anything.[24]

The letter is surprisingly joyless, given that at the time of writing it Conrad is about to marry or has only just married. Even so, one can imagine that he may have feared that marital life would mean a premature end to his new literary career – especially given the fact that he is at this point between projects, and not immersed in writing. The letter gives us a glimpse of Conrad in a raw and exposed moment, when he implicitly turns to Garnett for solace. The elements of modernity that he describes have potentially liberating possibilities from the novelist's point of view: the self as the negation of Platonic being gives way to stream-of-conscious narrative; deferred endings; incomplete character development; and aesthetic disunity, all of which contributed to something of a new *telos* for art in a post-teleological age, an era of endless "becoming."[25] So far, Conrad's relationship to modernism seems relatively conventional. However, his words suggest despair; they imply a desire for more than this – for a truth more substantial and reliable than a mere "fidelity to passing emotions." He is inviting Garnett to contest the ground of such hopelessness. Conrad knows futility; he may turn to Nietzsche to voice to his feelings – but pervading this epistolary gesture is a searching disposition rather than an attachment to the modern ideas he explores.[26]

Conrad's letters also include direct critiques of modern thought. Three years later in a letter to the emerging novelist John Galsworthy, Conrad shows just how careful he was to resist as far as possible an unthinking acceptance of a contemporary point of view. Conrad and Galsworthy enjoyed each other's ongoing, mutual support;[27] but at the inception of their friendship in 1897 Conrad mentored the younger writer. We can see Conrad's position as guide or teacher in the excerpt below where he defends Henry James against Galsworthy's cousin who has apparently tried to argue – in Conrad's words – that James "does not write from the heart":

> Yes, it is good criticism. Only I think that to say that Henry James does not write from the heart is maybe hasty [...] Technical perfection, unless there is some real glow to warm and illumine it from within, must necessarily be cold. I argue that in H.J. there is such a glow and not a dim one either, but to us used, absolutely accustomed to unartistic expression of fine, headlong, honest (or dishonest) sentiments the art does appear heartless. The outlines are so clear, the figures so finished, chiselled [*sic*.], carved and brought out that we exclaim, – we, used to the shades of contemporary

fiction, to the more or less malformed shades, – we exclaim, stone! Not at all. I say flesh and blood – very perfectly presented, – perhaps with too much perfection of *method*.[28]

Guiding Galsworthy away from the cousin-critic's judgment of James's work, Conrad frames his response with the tentative words "maybe" and "perhaps" while firmly addressing the folly of automatically associating "technical perfection" with coldness. He argues that contemporary sensibilities can blind readers to the humanity that radiates from James's exceptionally precise, carefully detailed narratives. His point is that modern readers may lack the subtly required to appreciate James's art, for they may tend to associate "unartistic" expression – an overt (but paradoxically artistic, intentional) inattention to method or craft – with authenticity. But Conrad avoids alienating Galsworthy by using the collective personal pronoun "we" to include himself among those readers who have become "absolutely accustomed to the more or less malformed shades" of contemporary styles. This makes his words all the more persuasive, for they communicate an all-encompassing outlook: Conrad is humble enough to empathize with the position he is attempting to critique; he is able to see and understand the world through another's eyes while guiding his reader to see the merits of a different point of view. Without saying so directly, he is arguing that a more perceptive eye – indeed a more discerning reader – would be able to recognize Henry James's warmth, that human "glow." To do justice to James, one must know how to read him. Conrad's non-didactic approach makes his reader see not only what he sees (a merely subjective point of view) but urges his reader to see as fully and deeply as possible.

Action ... Nothing but Action

To return to the excerpt from that pivotal letter to William Blackwood: Conrad calls himself modern, while in the same epistolary breath he differentiates his work from modern literature – claiming (again) that his fiction "is not an endless analysis of affected sentiments but in its essence it is action [...] nothing but action."[29] Action is a key concept by which Conrad distinguishes his project from literary modernism. Eloise Knapp Hay points out the centrality of action to Conrad's literary ethics, drawing from his essay "Books" where he writes that "literary creation being only one of the legitimate forms of human activity has no value but on the condition of not excluding the fullest recognition to all the more distinct forms of action."[30] Consider Conrad's passionate yet rational outlook: fiction "has no value but on" one condition, while writing is just one "human activity" among others. Is this the conceptual basis of Conrad's frame narratives – where we witness the external narrator's attempt to give "the fullest recognition" to the world of action, implicitly putting art (and the artist) in the service of life? Still, Conrad's claim to focus on action may be a bit puzzling, as critic Geoffrey Galt Harpham argues: "Other modern novelists, including Gide, Mann, James, Proust, and Woolf, also seem to devalue action, at least in comparison to Fielding, Dickens, Clemens, or Tolstoi, but the torpor of Conrad's works has a peculiar and distinctive quality."[31] When it comes to action and agency, Conrad differs in some degree from his eighteenth-century forebears; his older, nineteenth-century contemporaries; and his younger, modernist contemporaries. Even if we decide against taking Conrad at his own word (that he values action above all else), his novels at the very least refuse an *unqualified* association with literary modernism's devaluation of action.

It *is* worth taking Conrad at his word, however, not least because his letters show a preoccupation with the meaning and status of "action" that extends throughout his career. In a letter to Marcel Proust's English translator Charles Kenneth Scott Moncrieff – written almost one month after Proust's death, and twenty years after Conrad's emphatic declaration about action to Blackwood – Conrad responds to the translation of *Du coté de chez Swann*. He describes Proust as

> a writer who has pushed analysis to the point where it became creative. All that crowd of personages [...] are rendered visible to us by the force of analysis alone [...] Those who have found beauty in Proust's work are perfectly right. It is there [...] I don't think there ever has been in the whole of literature such an example of the power of analysis and I feel pretty safe in saying that there will never be another.[32]

With characteristic warmth, Conrad marvels at Proust's ability to make us see characters *without* action, for Proust depends mainly on the "force of analysis." We can recognize in Conrad's remarks the capacity to see beyond his own ambivalence towards "analysis" to express his appreciation of Proust's and by extension Moncrieff's unique achievement. In another part of the letter, Conrad asks "- how many descriptive lines have they got to themselves in the whole body of that immense work? Perhaps, counting the lines, half a page each."[33] Such an approach to literature is, Conrad remarks, entirely new. Proust reinvents the novel form – hence Virginia Woolf's praise upon reading him, "What remains to be written after that?"[34] *Du coté de chez Swann* is categorically modern in that it is different from what has come before and likely never to be repeated; it is also retrospectively modern in terms of early twentieth-century literary modernist practices, for it approaches characterization and the world of the novel with an inward-looking preoccupation that defies nineteenth-century critical categories of characterization and description.

While Conrad compliments Proust's achievement, we might heed the advice of Richard Curle who cautions that praise in Conrad's letters is often best read as an expression of good will to the writer – or, in this case, translator – rather than a high regard for the work itself.[35] We need to watch for signs of Conrad's true meaning. In this case, the letter reflects Conrad's keen sense of his audience – and, more generally, shows his relational approach to writing and thinking. Conrad does not direct, but rather implicitly guides, his reader to see better. He notably excludes himself when he refers to Proust's admirers in the third person: he intellectually understands but does not necessarily belong to "those who have found beauty in Proust's work." He compliments the uniqueness of Proust's style – but his claim that "there will never be another" is ambiguous, suggesting not only singular, unrepeatable genius but also that Proust takes novelty to an extreme.

Most important for this study, though, is the fact that Conrad brings to *Du coté de chez Swann* a relatively old formulation in identifying what makes this work so unique – for his comment on "analysis" in Proust refers to the pivotal letter to William Blackwood which Conrad wrote in 1902, about a decade before Proust published the first book of *À la recherche du temps perdus*. As we saw in that early letter, Conrad juxtaposes "endless analysis" with his own focus on "action [...] nothing but action." In his letter to Moncrieff, Conrad leaves out "endless" (i.e., without an end or *telos*) – and yet, it would be safe to assume that the term "analysis" – especially given its connotations of an intellectual activity that breaks down an object into parts – retains the suggestion of pointlessness, in both the colloquial and literal, anti-teleological senses of the word. Indeed, Conrad's self-conscious adherence to "action" speaks to a rift between ancient, teleological thought and modernity. However, to see this clearly and fully – to understand its importance – we must consider the Aristotelian parentage of Conrad's use of the word "action," and the status of this term in modern thought.

Conrad and Aristotle

Again, Conrad intentionally places "action [...] nothing but action" at the centre of his artistic vision – which he elaborates as an outlook on "human beings that will bleed to prick and are moving in a visible world." The force of Conrad's declared focus becomes especially apparent in Conrad's juxtaposition of his own interest in "action" and what he observes to be a characteristically modern "analysis of affected sentiments." For Conrad, action has to do with human beings as embodied agents – i.e., beings who are neither gods nor beasts, who are mortal (we "bleed to prick") and thus to an extent passive subjects, yet also "moving," capable of intentional actions in relation to a "visible" or real context. However, "action" also refers to an *idea* that unfolds through and unifies a work of art.

Conrad's distinction between "action" and an interest in "affected sentiments" recalls the quarrel between the ancients and the moderns. As Thomas Pfau explains in *Minding the Modern*, modern Western philosophy rejects the ancient Greeks' perspective on human beings as capable of self-aware, intentional actions that they could tenably subject to judgment. We see the famous quarrel play out in philosopher David Hume whose "atomist and naturalist" outlook on the human Nietzsche inherits.[36] Hume argues that the ancients were deluded to think that they could rationally deliberate about or dispute human action: all we can say for certain is that there are discrete physiological elements that contribute to our movements apparent to the senses; any deeper motivations remain unintelligible. Hume writes, "the ultimate actions of mankind can never, in any case, be accounted for by reason, but recommend themselves entirely to the sentiments and affections of mankind, without any dependence on the intellectual faculties."[37] Hume's diction ("never"; "entirely"; "without any") argues for an absolute division between action and reason; and between reason and emotion. He explains that "the distinct boundaries and offices of *reason* and *taste* are easily ascertained. The former conveys the knowledge of truth and falsehood: The latter gives the sentiment of beauty and deformity, vice and virtue,"[38] effectively limiting reason and knowledge to the realm of "facts." As I hope to show, Conrad refuses such extremes in an outlook that allows for "contingency and doubt [as] natural entailments of our manifestly imperfect modes of apprehension and cognition."[39] Indeed, Conrad seeks to preserve uncertainty as the condition of ethical action – where intention, deliberation, and prudence can take place "from within," giving us a vision of human beings as at least potentially intelligent and intelligible-enough agents. The intellectual trajectory – in this reading – between Hume and Nietzsche is important because the latter might seem, as a critic of modern moral complacency and as an admirer of the ancient Greeks, to be not just an analogue but a potential intellectual ally for Conrad. However, even though Conrad is critical of modernity in ways that sometimes recall Nietzsche (as we shall see, especially in chapters 2 and 4), Conrad's moderate outlook on nature and human nature, and his perspective on art, ultimately complicate a Nietzschean reading.[40]

In short, by contrasting a modern, "endless" (anti-teleological) interest in emotion with his own deliberate focus on "action" Conrad includes in his vision of things an implicitly classical dimension. In Aristotle's view, every action is "a purposeful action (or an action 'aimed at an end') based on a decision for which its agent is responsible."[41] In life as in art (ethics and aesthetics are one and the same for both Aristotle and Conrad), the ultimate "end" is happiness or human flourishing (*eudaimonia*); an idea of a specifically human good orients our deliberations about and appraisals of our actions, even as the conditions that allow us to realize our natures are subject to question.[42] Tragic figures miss the mark between excesses or competing demands on their loyalty; this appears to us as a failure because their action impedes human flourishing. In other words, when Aristotle refers to "action," he means not only the tragic figure's conduct or the events on stage but an underlying idea about human nature and the nature of reality that the play makes intelligible to us. We see this especially in Aristotle's famous definition of tragedy as "a representation of a serious, complete action which has magnitude [...] represented by people acting and not by narration; accomplishing by means of pity and terror the catharsis of such emotions."[43] When Aristotle refers to "a complete action" he means – as he explains later in the *Poetics* – that the action that unfolds through the play is for an audience in retrospect wondrously "necessary" and "probable"; as a result of tragic action the audience is reminded of an intelligible truth (or the truth) about the nature of human living.[44] Tragic action is "complete": it "ought to represent a single action, and a whole one at that"; every element of the play is "necessary and essential to the whole."[45] Thus "action" captures the aesthetic unity of the play which is not purely aesthetic at all, but rather something like a truthful construct, neither radical fabrication nor continuous with the particularities of experience.

Conrad's description of his artistic method recalls Aristotle's definition of "action" as a probable and necessary truth that unfolds in a work of fiction. Consider, for example, another letter to William Blackwood, in which Conrad writes about his approach to structure in a story, two novellas, and a major novel:

> In the light of the final incident, the whole story in all its descriptive detail shall fall into its place – acquire its value and its significance. This is my

method based on deliberate conviction. I've never departed from it. I
call your own kind self to witness and I beg to instance Karain – Lord
Jim (where the method is fully developed) – and the last pages of Heart
of Darkness where the interview of the man and the girl locks in – as it
were – the whole 30000 words of narrative description into one suggestive
view of a whole phase of life and makes of that story something quite on
another plane than an anecdote of a man who went mad in the Centre of
Africa. And Youth itself [...] exists only in virtue of my fidelity to the idea
and the method.[46]

Conrad appeals to Blackwood's character, his "kind self," in an effort
to guide the latter's interpretation. He compares "Karain: A Memory"
(1898); *Heart of Darkness* (1899); *Lord Jim: A Tale* (1900), and "Youth: A
Narrative" (1899), inviting Blackwood to recognize an underlying pattern as a purposeful aspect of his craft. The "final incident" in each
work reveals – or "locks in" – each story's "value and significance." The
formulation is comprehensive, including the character of the artist (his
"conviction" and "fidelity"), aesthetic form ("all the descriptive detail
shall fall into place"), meaning ("significance") and the moral purpose
of his art (its "value"). While most readers can see that his stories are
not merely entertaining "anecdotes," Conrad explains how or why this
is so: they manage to convey "one suggestive view of a whole phase
of life." Conrad argues that he does not simply relate an experience in
his fiction – but that literary narrative is itself a way of seeing that sug-
gestively *reveals* (or makes intelligible) an experience as a meaningful
"whole." When Conrad explains in the same letter to Blackwood that
"the idea in [*Heart of Darkness*] is not as obvious as in *youth* – or at least
not so obviously presented" and that this work "is a little wider – is less
concentrated upon individuals," he speaks to an "action" as an "idea"
about the nature of reality that works through the characters.[47]

Conrad sounds especially Aristotelian when, in his memoir *A Personal Record*, he overtly contrasts historical with literary narratives. He
asks, "And what is a novel if not a conviction of our fellow-men's existence strong enough to take upon itself a form of imagined life clearer
than reality and whose accumulated verisimilitude of selected epi-
sodes puts to shame the pride of documentary history?"[48] The novelist
aspires to convey an outlook that is deeper, more conscious or considered, less specifically personal or private than an individual's belief or
opinion. Similarly, in the *Poetics* Aristotle explains that tragic poetry
reveals human truths that would be otherwise difficult to recognize;
aesthetic unity, when considered from the perspective of an audience
or readership, has philosophical implications.[49] Amid the arbitrary or

irrational aspects of reality there are truths about the nature of human existence that tragedy aims to make intelligible by way of coherent, causal links internal to a plot. Indeed, Aristotle teaches that literature is more philosophical than history because "poetry tends to speak of universals, history of particulars. A universal is the sort of thing which a person may well do in accordance with probability or necessity."[50] Literature is more philosophical than history – more suited to representing "universals" – for it is not restricted to documenting circumstantial truths or facts, events as they truly occurred or people as they actually lived. Conrad's claim that art represents "our fellow-men's existence" is a gentler, less overtly political version of Aristotle's implicit defence of art's centrality to the *polis*; but with Aristotle, Conrad defends fiction's relative complexity and its inherent value by contrasting it with other genres of narrative and other disciplines, such as history. Just as Conrad's use of "verisimilitude" refers to more than a merely convincing or accurate portrayal of people and events, so it is that for Aristotle, *mimesis* or "imitation [...] is *not* mere replication"[51] but ventures into the ethical imagination where we meet with what truly *is* and what could possibly be.[52]

For Conrad, as for Aristotle, literature involves recovery work: tragedy returns citizens to a felt recognition of shared human truths – and in Conrad's literary credo, he claims that in his fiction readers may find "that truth for which [they] have forgotten to ask." If the novelist's "conscience is clear" – that is, if he remains true to the exigencies of his craft –

> his answer to those who in a fullness of a wisdom which looks for immediate profit [...] who demand to be promptly improved, or encouraged, or frightened, or shocked, or charmed must run thus: – My task which I am trying to achieve is, by the power of the written word, to make you hear, to make you feel – it is, before all, to make you *see*. That – and no more, and it is everything. If I succeed, you shall find there according to your deserts: encouragement, consolation, fear, charm – all you demand – and, perhaps, also that glimpse of truth for which you have forgotten to ask.
>
> To snatch a moment of courage, from the remorseless rush of time, a passing phase of life, is only the beginning of the task. The task approached in tenderness and faith is to hold up unquestioningly, without choice and without fear, the rescued fragment before all eyes in the light of a sincere mood.[53]

For Conrad as for Aristotle, literature saves us from being lost in a total immersion in life – in the inevitably blinding "remorseless rush of time" – by appealing to our capacity "to see," that is, to witness, understand, and recognize. In the midst of living, we may lose track of our desire for the truth – for that "glimpse" that escapes us anyway, given the relentless passage of time. Literature returns us to ourselves – and so, we readers can expect to be "improved" by a novel, but more deeply than we might think. The so-called improvement happens outside the crude economies of "profit" and "efficiency" and is therefore not "prompt" or immediate or easily observable, nor does it offer us a fact or conclusion that we can extract from the work and apply to the extra-literary world. Indeed, Conrad defends art's necessary escape from the consumer's language of use and gratification – a framework that precludes our coming to art for its own sake upon which, paradoxically, any real "benefit" would depend.[54] Instead, as Aristotle observes in the *Metaphysics*, "stories" have something to do with wonder – with the experience of *thaumazein*; we encounter in literature "that which endures forever." The absence of a final explication, description, or representation does not exclude the possibility of truth – but the truth with which Conrad is concerned has to do with human beings: we will see something truthful in his work, perhaps, about "courage" rather than the eternal things with which the ancient philosophers were concerned. A novel contains "all the truth of *life*."[55]

Conrad's greatest challenge as a modern novelist was to work with the disappearance of the omniscient narrator's authority without abandoning the truth. Our greatest challenge is to make sense of Conrad's complex vision, which comprises neither a reactionary rejection of modern thought nor a blind acceptance of it. As we have seen, Conrad's distinction between his own focus on "action [...] nothing but *action*" and "endless analysis" in modern fiction suggests an Aristotelian use of "action" as an underlying idea, or constellation of ideas, about human nature and the nature of reality that unfolds through a work of art. Conrad wants to convey our shared mortality (for we "bleed to prick") as an incontrovertible limit on our (nevertheless) considerable capacity for agency as we "move through a visible world." In the coming chapters, with the help of Aristotle, we will consider how Conrad evolves a passionately moderate voice and outlook, starting with his second novel, *An Outcast of the Islands* (1896), where he enlists the powerful tropes of ancient tragedy to critique modernity as an era of ideological and practical extremes.

2

An Outcast of the Islands: Tragedy, Pathos, and Conrad's Narrative Appeal

The old sea [...] was the sea before the time when the French mind set the Egyptian muscle in motion and produced a dismal but profitable ditch. Then a great pall of smoke sent out by the countless steam-boats was spread over the restless mirror of the Infinite. The hand of the engineer tore down the veil of the terrible beauty in order that greedy and faithless landlubbers might pocket dividends. The mystery was destroyed. Like all mysteries it lived only in the hearts of its worshippers. The hearts changed; the men changed [...] The sea of the past was an incomparably beautiful mistress, with inscrutable face, with cruel and promising eyes. The sea of to-day is a used-up drudge, wrinkled and defaced by the churned-up wakes of brutal propellers, robbed of the enslaving charm of its vastness, stripped of its beauty, of its mystery and its promise.[1]

The second chapter of *An Outcast of the Islands* (1896) opens with a moving commentary on the relentlessness of modern technological advancement. Presenting us with something of a panoramic view of the nineteenth century, the novel's unnamed narrator laments the shift from sail to steam and the opening of the Suez Canal in 1869. In this bitter yet eloquent description he contrasts a respectful love of nature's "mystery" with an apparent will – driven by greed – to master it. The mechanized, "countless[ly]" proliferating steamboats with the "brutal" churn of their propellers debase the majestic, "infinite" reflection of sky in sea. The narrator's anger and longing point to deeper feelings of helplessness before the march of history, as "the old sea" that extends back to the Greeks and the ancient world gives way to the "sea of to-day" and altogether "changed" human beings. History will have its way with all of us. And so, at the outset of the novel we wonder if the narrator's impassioned critique will leave us with something, anything tenable to affirm.

An Outcast of the Islands is the second work in Conrad's "Lingard" or "Malay" Trilogy, a group of novels that share a Malaysian setting and Captain Lingard, the adventurous English trader. All three novels – *Almayer's Folly: A Story of an Eastern River* (1895), *An Outcast* (1896), and *The Rescue: A Romance of the Shallows* which Conrad began writing in 1896 and completed in 1920[2] – possess the "tragic texture" that Michael Valdez Moses sees in many of Conrad's works.[3] *An Outcast*, however, stands out as a particularly ambitious work – a formative moment in Conrad's literary career. The first in the trilogy, *Almayer's Folly*, centres on one of Lingard's protégés, Dutch colonist Kaspar Almayer. In Almayer we witness not an ancient tragic hero's piteous and fearsome fall to misfortune but the protagonist's foolish deterioration from misery to destruction. *Almayer's Folly* does contain a hero of the classical variety: Nina's beloved noble warrior-prince Dain successfully negotiates a genuine ethical conflict between personal love and honour, with the suggestion of future happiness for the couple beyond the scope of the novel and outside an increasingly modernized world. Reinforcing this idea is Lingard's role in the final book, *The Rescue*. Here, Lingard is caught between a political commitment to restoring his friend Prince Hassim to power in Wajo, and an erotic entanglement with British aristocrat Mrs. Edith Travers. Lingard proves unable to navigate between love and politics: he fails Hassim and in doing so fails to realize his deepest desire of honour. Even so, the status of Lingard's apparent tragedy is debatable, as Allan Simmons's commentary suggests: "While the backdrop of revolutionary instability in *The Rescue* provides a fitting context for the encounter between Lingard and Edith Travers, the sheer difference in scale between background and foreground renders the latter myopically self-serving."[4] If Simmons is correct that the novel presents love as trivial in comparison to politics, then there is no genuine tragic conflict such as we see, if only briefly, in Dain of *Almayer's Folly*. And even if *The Rescue* does value personal love and politics equally, the novel bids farewell to ancient tragedy – for its position in the chronology of the trilogy makes us aware that Lingard is at his most classically heroic in the distant past.

It is in *An Outcast*, however, where we witness Captain Lingard's *real* tragedy – where he nobly tries to save someone who turns out not to be worth the effort after all. The novel is structured by two characters and crises between which the narrator invites us to distinguish. In the initial crisis, Lingard's protégé Peter Willems – a pathetic 30-year-old white Dutch trading clerk with Hudig & Co. in Macassar – has stolen from his employer to pay for gambling debts and some unexpected expenses. Before Willems has finished replacing the money, he is discovered and fired – and he is rejected by his wife Joanna who is also his employer's daughter. Lingard admonishes Willems but intends to make things right again with Hudig and Joanna while the humiliated clerk stays with Lingard's other protégé, Kaspar Almayer, who manages the captain's trading post in Sambir. Intended as a temporary escape from controversy, Sambir instead turns out to be a high-stakes sphere of action where Willems falls in love with Aïssa, the beautiful daughter of the elderly Arab chief Omar el Badavi. When Almayer refuses to help Willems set up his own trading post across the river, Willems is indignant and commits a second crime: he shares with Arab trader Syed Abdulla the location of Lingard's "secret river," the mysterious passage that is the source of Lingard's monopoly over trade in the region. Lingard returns to Sambir with Joanna and her infant son, hoping to reunite the family; however, upon learning of Willems's actions, the captain confronts and banishes his emaciated, delusional protégé to the island. Unenthusiastic at the prospect of living indefinitely near Willems, Almayer sends Joanna and the baby to Willems's camp to facilitate an escape – but when mother and child arrive, Aïssa is shocked to discover that Willems is already married – and shoots him to death.

An Outcast of the Islands belongs to those philosophical works of fiction that, according to Terry Eagleton, borrow tropes of ancient tragedy to offer a "displaced critique of modernity."[5] If, as Eagleton claims, tragic poetry will always "imply an [...] evaluation of its objects,"[6] *An Outcast* inherits that critical, evaluative work. In what follows, Aristotle's theory of tragedy – including the tragic figure and the aspects of reversal (*peripeteia*); recognition (*anagnorisis*); and catharsis – will provide us with a framework within which to recognize the novel's critique of modern extremes and Conrad's response: the early formation of a compassionate yet rational narrator who might guide the reader's judgment. David Gallop's gloss on Aristotle's "hamartia" is instructive, here: the term does not mean flaw, exactly, but rather "missing the mark" of right action between extremes in a given context.[7] We witness the hero's error in judgment with pity and fear – seeing our own human possibilities in his fall. This perspective contrasts with modern pathos, where human agency is an illusion; all we have is the levelling truth of radical uncertainty and eternally disputable constructs that help us to avoid seeing the futility of our actions. Peter Willems comes to embody modern pathos, especially in the moments before his death when he realizes "the horror of bewildered life where he could understand nothing and nobody round him; where he could guide, control, comprehend nothing and no one – not even himself."[8] However, the unnamed narrator and Captain Lingard together begin to suggest an alternative to this bewildering endlessness despite the disappearing "old sea."

Tragic Figures, Ancient and Modern

Critics Leonard Orr and Claude Maisonnat both conclude that Peter Willems's character is so contemptible as to render the *Poetics* irrelevant to the novel.[9] They explain that Willems cannot undergo a tragic fall from greatness because he is too ignoble to begin with. However, Orr and Maisonnat both read Aristotle's theory as a formal standard against which we might measure the novel's success, rather than a field of ideas within which Conrad implicitly worked. In Conrad's novels we meet with ordinary characters such as Captain Whalley of *The End of the Tether* (1902), a literally and figuratively blind merchant seaman whose desperate actions are driven by a blind devotion to his daughter; and in *The Secret Agent* (1907), Winnie Verloc, a married woman living on the margins of London society, finally takes action by killing her husband when, divested of every illusion – but primarily the illusion that her husband could be a father to her brother Stevie – she realizes that Verloc is responsible for Stevie's death. Thus Conrad's tragic characters are not restricted, as Aristotle would have it, to "those people with a great reputation and good fortune, e.g. Oedipus, Thyestes and distinguished men from similar families."[10] Rather, in Conrad's fiction we encounter ordinary people who nevertheless compel our admiration because of their intrinsic qualities of character, their commitments and loyalties, and their actions in extreme situations and psychological states.

Along with many of Conrad's other potentially tragic protagonists, *An Outcast*'s Peter Willems – with his humble beginnings in a poor, motherless family in Rotterdam – suggests a modernization of, or egalitarian take on, Aristotle's theory of tragedy. Still, the *Nicomachean Ethics* teaches readers to value social esteem and wealth only insofar as they increase opportunities for the exercise of the virtues (such as generosity) in the unobstructed way that constitutes happiness.[11] Similarly, the *Poetics* emphasizes not the tragic figure's social status but his or her character and humanity: "such a person is one who is neither superior [to us] in virtue and justice, nor undergoes a change to misfortune because of some vice or wickedness, but because of some error."[12] An audience will be merely repulsed by the fall of a wholly virtuous character, and we may be hard-pressed to feel pity and fear for an entirely vicious character who suffers. In other words, Aristotle's theory excludes characters who would elicit either intense veneration or disgust – and in so doing, teaches that tragedy's ethical force comes from its portrayal of neither gods nor beasts, but of human beings who are by nature sub-ject to error and misfortune – that is, to chance, risk, and accident. This certainly applies to Willems who is hardly at risk of being "preeminent in virtue and justice." Although he often acts impulsively and can be cruel, he is too obviously foolish and blind to qualify as a purely evil character, at least on Aristotle's terms. After all, Lingard does at first single out Willems as someone worth saving. Indeed, the fact that Wil-lems has abandoned the "commonplace story" of his life in Rotterdam suggests a dissatisfaction with the ordinary and potentially admirable desire to somehow rise above it.[13] Also, Lingard sees concrete examples of potential excellence in his protégé, finding that the youth "wrote a beautiful hand, became soon perfect in English, was quick at figures" and that "as he grew older his trading instincts developed themselves astonishingly."[14] All of these qualities have affinities with a genuinely tragic figure.

And yet, the classically tragic hero must have risen to greatness through virtuous actions, only to fall from achieved greatness because of an error in judgment. This trajectory appears in Captain Lingard's story – albeit in the margins of the novel and increasingly in the margins of history. We read that Lingard is driven by the elevated pleasures of exploring the world and discovering new materials to trade, of extend-ing his knowledge and wisdom. He enjoys discovery for its own sake – an adventurer's version of Aristotle's highest pleasure of intellect or contemplation. We also read of Lingard's "straightforward simplicity of motive and honesty of aim,"[15] with an emphasis on the latter virtue – for soon afterwards the narrator tells us that Lingard "was liked [...] for his reckless generosity, for his unswerving honesty."[16] Indeed Lingard's character includes a matrix of virtues:

> He loved [the sea] with the ardent affection of a lover, he made light of it with the assurance of perfect mastery, he feared it with the wise fear of a brave man, and he took liberties with it as a spoiled child might do with a paternal and good-natured ogre. He was grateful to it with the grati-tude of an honest heart. His greatest pride lay in his profound conviction of its faithfulness – in the deep sense of his unerring knowledge of its treachery.[17]

Lingard possesses bravery, gratitude, faithfulness, and an "unerringly" realistic knowledge of the sea; he embodies the very nature of the vir-tues as they become seamlessly integrated into one's character over time in a sphere of action. Lingard's settled character is such that he "naturally" (according to his "second" nature) feels and acts in a way that suits the object of his feelings: he fears the sea "with the wise fear of a brave man," which is to say that Lingard's experiences have educated or shaped his instinctive and natural fear of danger into a respectful fear of the sea.

The unnamed narrator conveys the limits of Lingard's "omniscience" – his knowledge and insight – without negating his moral authority. The tragic hero's admirability is not destroyed by his error in judgment, an error to which we are all potentially subject. In the aftermath of the first crisis, we witness Lingard's worldliness and knowledge, his generosity, and his command of human affairs. Lingard is shocked to learn that Willems was unaware that his wife is in fact Hudig's daughter – that Willems did not know his professional success is partly contingent on this domestic arrangement. Lingard responds with compassion for Willems and takes command of the situation by settling Willems's debt, placating Joanna, and removing the young clerk to Sambir for six weeks while the crisis ostensibly passes. As both men prepare to step into the boat that will ferry them to Lingard's ship, Lingard justifies his decision to help his disgraced protégé: "'You see,' he went on, argumentatively, fumbling about the top of the lamp 'you got yourself so crooked amongst those 'longshore quill-drivers that you could not run clear in any way. That's what comes of such talk as yours and of such a life. A man sees so much falsehood that he begins to lie to himself.'"[18] Lingard's "fumbling" suggests an awkwardness in handling the situation and the truth. He is not exactly naïve: he knows what Willems values most, commenting that Willems could have had a different life at "sea, my boy, the sea! But you never would; didn't think there was enough money in it; and now – look!"[19] It's just that Willems lies outside the scope of Lingard's morality. The captain cannot see – and would not suspect – that when he promises Willems that he will set everything right with Joanna, and to "Trust me!," Willems quietly "smile[s] in the darkness."[20] The sinister aspect of Willems's covertly self-satisfied smile is confirmed when we learn that Willems has been planning to share any information he might glean about Lingard's "secret river" with Hudig.[21] Thus the narrator leads us to see what Lingard could not fathom at the time – which is that Willems is inherently loyal only to himself. Still, the narrator tells us that "Lingard led the way down the steps, swinging the lamp and speaking over his shoulder," suggesting that there is something to be glimpsed in those flashes of light.[22] Lingard's character remains a guide, however flawed, through the darkness.

By contrast, at the novel's outset the narrator makes it clear that Willems has only delusions of grandeur: "He believed in his genius and in his knowledge of the world. Others should know of it also. For their own good and for his greater glory."[23] If the young trading clerk takes himself so seriously that he lectures his colleagues, the narrator's imagery diminishes this grandiose self-image. We read, for example, that "in the afternoon he expounded his theory of success over the little tables [...] The billiard balls stood still as if listening also."[24] Willems may consider himself important, but his sphere of influence is "little"; and his audience is as conscious of his teachings as the "billiard balls."[25] In addition, Willems believes himself to be a generous provider for his family – while the narrator makes it clear that he only condescends to support his wife and her extended family, the DaSouzas, while he uses their dependence as an easy means of exercising power. The narrator gives us insight into what Lingard cannot see – Willems's telling private conduct – especially in his wife Joanna's "frightened eyes" as she watches her drunken husband "sprawled in the long chair."[26] When Willems loses his job, family, and social position as a result of this (albeit petty) crime, we can see that his so-called fall only mocks the fall of a real hero.

If he doesn't fit the profile of a classically tragic figure, Willems isn't classically comedic, either. As Aristotle explains, while tragic poetry centres on a character whose status and virtues compel our admiration, comedy portrays someone who is "laughable" given his or her "error and ugliness that is not painful and destructive."[27] There is a certain levity attached to ancient comedy that does not fit with Willems's story: we are not tempted to laugh at his demise – for his actions are increasingly painful to witness, having serious consequences not only for his own life but also for the lives of other characters. And while his reproachable figure may at times seem cynically comedic given the gulf between reality and his sense of it, the novel certainly explores the serious depths of human suffering. One would even hesitate to classify *An Outcast* as a tragicomedy given the catastrophic outcome of Willems's actions. Instead, we get an absurdist tragicomedy that lacks the laughter that modern dramatists such as Samuel Beckett, for example, will evoke.

The narrator overtly mocks Willems's conception of himself as a quasi-overman – signalling what J.H. Stape calls *An Outcast*'s critique of "extreme subjectivity."[28] We see this, for example, in a passage of free indirect discourse from the novel's first chapter where Willems reflects on his successful negotiation, "by sheer pluck," of a rather shady-sounding firearms deal: "That was the way to get on. He disapproved of the elementary dishonesty that dips the hand in the cash-box, but one could evade the laws and push the principles of trade to their furthest consequences. Some call that cheating. Those are the fools, the weak, the contemptible. The wise, the strong, the respected have no scruples.

Where there are scruples there can be no power."[29] To Willems's mind, the truly admirable – "the respected" – are those who have the mettle and cleverness to circumvent laws and transgress moral principles. He disdains "elementary dishonesty" because it shows the moral weakness of the person who hasn't the will to "push" his dishonesty "to [its] furthest consequences." In an apparent attempt to reject what sounds much like Nietzsche's slave morality, Willems professes that "the wise" know that "scruples" or principles prevent us from achieving excellence or "winning." Only the foolish and "the weak" will follow the rules.

Despite what he may tell himself, though, Willems is supreme only to the extent that he is supremely conventional. For example, Willems's theory or "doctrine of success" is obviously trivial: "How good was life for those that were on the winning side. He had won the game of life – also the game of billiards."[30] This conception of life as a game reduces morality to a system of rules put in play or a construct without any referent beyond itself: the game defines what winning and losing entail – and conveniently ignores the humbling role of chance in any game. His conventionality is particularly apparent when we see him through the eyes of tertiary figures such as "the Chinaman marker" who "would lean wearily against the wall, [...] his eyelids dropped in the drowsy fatigue of late hours and in the buzzing monotony of the unintelligible stream of words poured out by the white man."[31] Willems's ideas, his speeches, are so ironically monotonous, so dull, that they lull an audience to sleep – and the narrator sympathetically captures an observer's privately ironic insight into Willems's racist assumption of superiority.[32]

Willems's ironic conventionality ultimately defeats him, keeps him from the kind of happiness that (again) Nina and Dain achieve at *Almayer's Folly*'s end. When he falls in love with Aïssa in Sambir, Willems cannot escape his prejudice – the same that caused him to view his wife's family as "those degenerate descendants of Portuguese conquerors."[33] As he explains to Almayer, Willems expects to take Aïssa away from her family and culture: "I would have her all to myself and away from her people – all to myself – under my own influence – to fashion – to mould – to adore – to soften – to…Oh! Delight! And then – then go away to some distant place where, far from all she knew, I would be all the world to her! All the world to her!"[34] This fantasy – recalling Almayer's own clichéd and futile vision for his biracial daughter Nina – reflects Willems's limited imagination and his settled, stubborn misogyny and racism. He is pathetic in part because he simply repeats the stereotypical traits of the European colonialist, and his character remains untouched by what might have been a transformative encounter.

We may seem at this point to encounter a contradiction in *An Out-cast*, between Willems's vacuous egotism as an implicit parody of Nietzsche's overman – as Conrad himself condemns Nietzsche's "mad individualism" – and a potentially Nietzschean take on conventions.[35] However, the apparent contradiction sheds light on a point of contact between Aristotle and Nietzsche, and opens the way to a deeper Aris-totelian reading of the novel. Both philosophers critique rule-bound actions and celebrate excellence, but Aristotle argues that ethics, given the wide range of situations one might encounter, requires an intrinsic capacity for good judgment, whereas for Nietzsche there is no truthful rational foundation for ethics: beneath mere appearances human nature is chaos thus beyond cognition.[36] *An Outcast*'s first sentence gives voice to both outlooks, expressing a wariness of adhering too closely to any moral system: "When he stepped off the straight and narrow path of his peculiar honesty, it was with an inward assertion of unflinching resolve to fall back again into the monotonous but safe stride of virtue as soon as his little excursion into the wayside quagmires had produced the desired effect."[37] In this passage of free indirect discourse, the nar-rator is also present, guiding our interpretation of Willems by moving towards and then veering away from moral judgment. For example, the narrator's reference to Willems's "path of honesty" echoes Aristotle's *Politics* where we read that "he who departs from the path of virtue will never be able to go sufficiently straight."[38] This echo amplifies the narrator's irony, making us see that Willems was foolish to believe he could steal without consequence; the chapter's closing words support this judgment, where the narrator's sarcasm speaks to the Aristotelian argument that character is the result of habituation, that actions shape character:[39] "true, he was conscious of a slight deterioration."[40] More-over, Willems's honesty is "peculiar," suggesting that he is honest on his own terms, which is hardly honesty at all. Even so, the narrative alters and fragments Aristotle's "path of virtue": "the path of honesty," although "straight," is "narrow," just as the passage aligns "virtue" with monotony or a dull obedience. At this early point in the novel, the narrator ironizes Willems's pathetic underestimation of the character-shaping effects of conduct, while simultaneously resisting a simplistic or unthinking application of a moral script to any life.

Tragic Reversal and the Pathos of Repetition

The narrator mocks Willems's belief that he can always "fall back again into the monotonous but safe stride of virtue as soon as his little excur-sion into the wayside quagmires had produced the desired effect."[41]

However, it is not specifically Willems's *fall* to which the novel initially draws attention, but his confidence that with the right attitude or "resolve" he can always "fall *back again*" or repeatedly return to the way things were. In other words, Willems imagines he has godlike powers – including the ability to overcome the limits of reality, limits that are uncovered by the work of tragedy. Aristotle refers to the limits of action in the *Nicomachean Ethics* by quoting the poet Agathon who writes, "For of this alone even god is deprived,/To make undone whatever things have been done."[42] The obverse of time's relentless passage is that this natural limit helps us keep in view the significance of our actions, especially our capacity to further or hinder happiness. This outlook recalls Aristotle's examples of *peripeteia* or tragic reversal in the *Poetics*, where we read that "the man who comes to delight Oedipus, and to rid him of his terror about his mother, does the opposite by revealing who Oedipus is"; and "Lynceus is being led to his death, and Danaus follows to kill him, but it comes about as a result of the preceding actions that Danaus is killed and Lynceus is rescued."[43] Willems's life of endless repetition pushes Aristotle's examples of reversal – and the natural limits they reveal – to a modern extreme.

Although Willems is physically exploring new terrain when he enters the island's interior, he ends up helplessly repeating his previous "excursion" into the "quagmires" of theft in Sambir, only on a much larger scale:

> Here and there he could see the beginnings of chopped-out pathways and with the fixed idea of getting out of sight of the busy river he would land and follow the narrow and winding path, only to find that it led nowhere, ending abruptly, in the discouragement of thorny thickets. He would go back slowly with a bitter sense of unreasonable disappointment and sadness, oppressed by the hot smell of earth, dampness and decay in that forest which seemed to push him mercilessly back into the glittering sunshine of the river: and he would recommence paddling with tired arms to seek another opening, to find another deception.[44]

The narrator echoes the novel's opening paragraph where Willems steps off his preferred "straight and narrow path of his peculiar honesty" – the path to which he intends to return without anyone detecting his detour into the "quagmires" of theft.[45] Now Willems follows a "winding" path, indicating a more complex or circuitous way than before – although the path is still "narrow," and leads to painful difficulties or "thorny thickets." That is, he remains restricted to his usual behaviour, informed by the "fixed idea" that leads to yet "another deception." The narrator repeats the word "narrow" to describe Willems's chosen foot-paths, including the pathway that "narrowed again" before leading to a "narrow way" – a succinct projection of what ultimately precludes Willems's happiness: his narrow-minded view of Aïssa. The repetition has two important implications, the most obvious of which is that it emphasizes futility: nothing is changing for Willems, except that he keeps making mistakes in a downward spiral towards self-destruction. The extreme irony of Willems's situation would have been too pessimistic for Aristotle; on the other hand, the shift from the metaphorical reference to "the path of honesty" to the subsequent description of pathways and footpaths suggests an Aristotelian shift in the narrative onto an intelligible ground of nature, including human nature.

Willems is not the admirable classical hero of ancient tragedy who misses the mark of right action due to an error in judgement. Instead, he is a figure of modern pathos who tries to avoid – that is, to overcome – the reality of choices, who tries to nullify choice altogether. Moreover, his denial of the limits revealed by reversal masks a deeper desire for an impossible, final "return" to a point where origin and end are indistinguishable.[46] When waiting for Aïssa at their meeting place, for example, Willems "felt soothed and lulled into forgetfulness of the past, into indifference as to his future [...] He lay very quiet, with all the ardour of desire running in his voice and shining in his eyes while his body was still like death itself."[47] Even this condition of stasis, so irresistible to Willems, becomes yet another imposition of a limit that he feels compelled to avoid. Indeed, he is unable to fully commit to Aïssa, even after he decides to sever ties with Almayer:

> As, with the sound of Almayer's laughter in his ears, he urged his canoe in a slanting course across the rapid current, *he tried to tell himself that he could return at any moment.* He would just go and look at the place where they used to meet, at the tree under which he lay when she took his hand, at the spot where she sat by his side. *Just go there and then return* – nothing more; but when his little skiff touched the bank he leaped out forgetting the painter and the canoe hung for a moment amongst the bushes and then swung out of sight before he had time to dash into the water and secure it. He was thunderstruck at first. *Now he could not go back.*[48]

The prospect of a future with Aïssa immediately turns into yet another demand against the opposite possibility – that Willems rejoin Almayer to wait for Lingard as planned, and Willems refuses to choose either possibility. If we have not yet reached the event of Willems's literal death, the narrator equates the denial of nature's limits with a figurative or moral death, for Willems "gives up – because the swamped craft is gone from under his feet, because the night is dark and the shore is far; because death is better than strife."[49] He may try to define himself as entirely passive, allowing the canoe to float away as if by accident. And yet, the narrator makes us see that, paradoxically, this passivity is itself a choice (and that choice is in fact inescapable): Willems chooses "death" over struggle or "strife."

It comes as no surprise, then, that Willems would try to evade responsibility for his treachery. Rather than suffer horror or even remorse at his resentful actions against Almayer and especially Lingard, "he had, for a moment, a wicked pleasure in the thought that what he had done could not be undone. He had given himself up. He felt proud of it. He was ready to face anything, to do anything. He cared for nothing, for nobody."[50] Feebly echoing Zarathustra's "Thus I willed it,"[51] Willems asserts his passivity while telling himself – again – that "he had given himself up." He is no longer constrained by his attachment to Lingard, and revels in the quasi-Dionysian pleasure of destroying the mere appearance of loyalty, the conventional bonds that cover over the truth that those bonds are groundless constructs. But the narrator guides our reading of the apparent revelry, reminding us that Willems only "thought himself very fearless. As a matter of fact he was only drunk; drunk with the poison of passionate memories" of his first encounter with Aïssa.[52] Willems isn't closer to life itself. In fact, his apparent fearlessness is an illusion that barely conceals the truth. If Willems finally comes up against the tragic structure of time and the irrevocability of action, he does not – or cannot – recognize it.

Recognition – Ancient and Modern

Willems's experiences of recognition are not always false or misguided, but their status is often ambiguous given the ease and consistency with which he returns to his customary state of blindness. In the *Poetics*, *anagnōrisis* or recognition – "a change from ignorance to knowledge"– exposes the probability and necessity of the tragic figure's suffering; what the hero experiences as an unexpected fall is revealed in this transition or *metabasis* as part of a larger, causal pattern.[53] As Stephen Halliwell explains, tragic figures (along with their audience) come to see the underlying order of things: "Recognition involves ignorance by definition, which again allows for – and once ignorance is part of action necessarily leads to – [active], positive error, as opposed to a merely passive state of erroneous belief."[54] Seeing the truth is unqualifiedly "positive" because it involves (according to

Aristotle) the highest human faculty of the intellect, but also because it returns the audience to the world with a renewed sense of the natural limits that shape human character, govern action, and enable human beings to flourish. Willems, by contrast, undergoes many fleeting moments of vision or quasi-realization from which he draws no real sustenance. Thus, against Aristotle's description of the hero's transition from ignorance to knowledge, Willems's repeated failures to see appear particularly significant: he is a shadow of the ancient hero, but also an expression of Conrad's scepticism about the possibility of positive knowledge and genuine heroism in the modern world – an ironic, philosophical outlook that anticipates *Heart of Darkness* and, as we shall see in the next chapter, *Lord Jim: A Tale*.

Given that the narrator introduces Willems as "the ignorant man," the novel self-consciously mirrors the structure of tragedy,[55] seemingly preparing the way for a scene of *anagnōrisis* or recognition, while hinting at its imminent subversion by emphasizing Willems's witlessness: "He experienced that irresistible impulse to impart information which is inseparable from gross ignorance. There is always some one thing which the ignorant man knows and that thing is the only thing worth knowing; it fills the ignorant man's universe. Willems knew all about himself [...] He believed in his genius and in his knowledge of the world. Others should know of it also. For their own good and for his greater glory."[56] Unlike the tragic figure whose settled character is decent and whose mistaken actions arise from an error in judgment, Willems's ignorance is pervasive – and the elevating experience of wonder is beyond his reach. He inherently parodies, as if to embody the impossibility of, fulfilling the maxims inscribed in Apollo's temple at Delphi, "Know thyself!" and "nothing in excess." His ignorance situates him for a fall – and yet he ends up undermining the classical expectation that he will, upon suffering misfortune, experience a change to knowledge, a clarifying moment of recognition not only of the causal pattern that led to his fall, but also a full realization that we are all both vulnerable and responsible agents. In the aftermath of his dismissal, immediately following his descent from professional success to humiliation, Willems reflects on his situation:

> As the sound of Hudig's insults that lingered in his ears grew fainter by the lapse of time, the feeling of shame was replaced slowly by a passion of anger against himself and still more against the stupid concourse of circumstances that had driven him into his idiotic indiscretion. Idiotic indiscretion; that is how he defined his guilt to himself. Could there be anything worse from

the point of view of his undeniable cleverness? What a fatal aberration of an
acute mind. He did not recognize himself there.[57]

Although Willems contemptuously reflects on "the stupid concourse
of circumstances that had driven him to his idiotic indiscretion," he is,
in his characterization of the events, still shielding himself from the
truth and from responsibility by situating himself as a passive victim:
"circumstances [...] had driven" him to theft. According to his rational-
izations, it was his "acute mind" that failed him; what matters to him
is not the morally deleterious action itself, but rather the fact that he
failed to fulfil his goal: he should have exercised more discretion. If
only he had been more careful, more strategic, he would have won the
game.[58] Willems thus shows how reason can lead one astray – but this
failure suggests not only a modern critique of reason, but also a failure
to reason well.[59] Against Willems's negative example we realize what
moment of *true* recognition would have looked like: a courageous
acknowledgment or pursuit of the truth in dialogue with Lingard. As
the word re-cognition or *ana* (again, back) *gnorisis* (making known) or
indicates, the tragic figure undergoes a return to, or recovery of, what
is; and the narrator's deeply ironic claim that Willems "did not recognize himself there" points to the layers of self-deception that can
preclude such recovery work.

The novel's historicist challenge, however, is to understand, through
Willems's example, modernity's outlook on recognition. In the aftermath of the discovery of his theft, Willems is rejected by his professional
community and his family. He drifts through Macassar:

> Another man was coming back. A man without a past, without a future, yet
> full of pain and shame and anger. He stopped and looked around. A dog or
> two glided across the empty street and rushed past him with a frightened
> snarl. He was now in the midst of the Malay quarter whose bamboo houses
> hidden in the verdure of their little gardens were dark and silent. Men,
> women and children slept in there. Human beings. Would he ever sleep
> and where? He felt as if he was the outcast of all mankind and as he looked
> hopelessly round, before resuming his weary march, it seemed to him that
> the world was bigger, the night more vast and more black.[60]

The narrator dramatizes the birth of the modern literary figure of the
outcast. Unlike the tragic hero who retrospectively sees a causal pattern of events and, more deeply the wondrous natural order of things,
Willems sees only a vaster and darker world. Whereas ancient tragedy
implicitly returns human beings to the *polis* with a renewed sense of

shared humanity, Willems can see only because he has been stripped bare of communal ties. There seems to be no middle ground here between an illusorily ordered world or context and the irrational over which it hovers. The villagers may have their community, but they are literally *and* figuratively asleep. The price of awareness, that state of being "awake" that Willems experiences in the present, fleeting moment, is (deluded) domestic happiness. Exile is the condition of insight. For the modern outcast, the truth is absent ancient wonder; to be awake is to face interminable darkness, a radically incomprehensible world.

Even so, Willems's emergence as the outcast implies a critique of this figure's extreme individualism. Perhaps the world only *appears* to be "more vast and more black." The narrator suggests that Willems's true moment of recognition occurs when "the respect and admiration of them all, the old habits and old affections finished abruptly in the clear perception of the cause of [Willems's] disgrace. He saw all this; and for a time he came out of himself, out of his selfishness – out of the constant preoccupation of his interests and his desires – out of the temple of self and the concentration of personal thought."[61] This genuine moment of recognition might seem to contradict J.H. Stape's claim that Willems "lacks an ability to perceive or affirm values or responsibilities beyond or outside those founded upon himself."[62] However, the point of the scene is not to reveal something new about Willems's character or to unsettle our understanding of it. Instead, the scene clarifies our critical appraisal of Willems. We come to see the shallowness of his despair and loneliness: they arise from self-worship, from a paradoxically self-defeating "concentration of personal thought," an intense preoccupation with one's own "interests and desires." Such insularity leads to the "endless analysis" which, as we saw in chapter 1, Conrad critiques in his letter William Blackwood.

At the novel's end, Conrad revisits this critique of insularity and solipsism – further ironizing the "concentration of personal thought." The narrator describes the moments before Willems's death:

> He looked without seeing anything – thinking of himself. Before his eyes the light of the rising sun burst above the forest with the suddenness of an explosion. He saw nothing. Then, after a time, he murmured with conviction – speaking half aloud to himself in the shock of the penetrating thought:
> "I am a lost man."
> He shook his hand above his head in a gesture careless and tragic, then walked down into the mist that closed above him in shining undulations under the first breath of the morning breeze.[63]

In a novel that esteems sight and insight, however sceptically – the narrator and Lingard both demonstrate the possibilities and human limits of seeing – the claim that Willems "looked without seeing anything" is particularly damning, as is the narrator's juxtaposition of the "explosion" of sunlight that occurs "before his [very] eyes" and Willems's final "penetrating thought." The sunrise illuminates the narrator's irony. That Willems is a "lost man" is hardly a dramatic revelation, but the passage also contains a philosophical idea: Willems – if we accept that he is a prototypically modern figure – is so morally disoriented or "lost" because he is blind to, or alienated from, nature. Willems's final "tragic" gesture is merely a performance of tragedy as he descends into the mist; and yet the imagery implies hope: the mist's "shining undulations under the first breath of a morning breeze" gives us the promise of the new day and capture nature's lasting beauty.[64]

Catharsis, Justice, and Modern Remonstrance

The confrontation between Willems and Lingard at *An Outcast*'s end dramatizes the distance between modern pathos and ancient tragedy – making us distinguish between a genuine, noble crisis and a pitiful crisis centred on the self. Despite his human failings, Lingard's crisis is admirable as he confronts an assault on his sense of justice. By contrast, Willems appears transparently self-serving as he desperately fights to maintain his misguided sense of self while continuing to deceive Lingard. Whereas Aristotle's tragic figure in the *Poetics* is answerable to his or her actions, Willems pathetically evades responsibility right to the end. If we are seeking a genuine tragedy on Aristotle's elevating, restorative terms, we must follow Lingard's example; Willems leaves us only with futility. To that end, Aristotle helps us to read the allusions to tragedy in the novel's final scenes and recognize the novel's appeal to our capacity to appraise character and conduct. Fiction – by way of a narrator as our guide – can make us *see*.

Conrad structures the novel's end by juxtaposing Willems's self-serving account of events with Lingard's profound crisis not only about his own material losses but about his sense of justice. Willems tries to claim that he never stole but rather borrowed from Hudig, and has – as Willems absurdly says twice – "always lived a virtuous life."[65] In an overtly ironic echo of the *Poetics*, Willems repeats three times that his original theft was "an error of judgement."[66] This is an implicit misappropriation of *hamartia* and a distraction from Willems's most egregious, second betrayal – especially since Lingard forgave Willems for the theft long ago, and promised to repair the damage. When Lingard echoes the phrase "an error of judgement" in "a blank tone," he amplifies Willems's monstrous understatement. The devastating outcome of Lingard's decision to trust Willems confirms what the narrator reveals at the outset of the novel: Willems's sole allegiance is to wealth and power; he can and will do anything to secure his own interests. This has material implications for Lingard – but it also throws him into a philosophical crisis: the betrayal leads him to doubt his orderly conception of universe.

By confronting Willems, Lingard courageously confronts the painful possibility that existence is fundamentally incomprehensible. After Lingard strikes Willems across the face, Willems explains, "I stood in the doorway long enough to pull a trigger – and you know I shoot straight." In response to this pathetic attempt to take the moral high ground, Lingard claims, "'You would have missed,' adding, 'There is, under heaven, such a thing as justice.'" Then again,

> the sound of that word [justice] on [Lingard's] own lips made him pause, confused, like an unexpected and unanswerable rebuke. The anger of his outraged pride, the anger of his outraged heart had gone out in the blow and there remained nothing but the sense of some immense infamy; of something vague, disgusting and terrible which seemed to surround him on all sides, hover about him with shadowy and stealthy movements like a band of assassins in the darkness of vast and unsafe places. Was there – under heaven – such a thing as justice? He looked at the man before him with such an intensity of prolonged glance that he seemed to see right through him, that at last he saw but a floating and unsteady mist in human shape. Would it blow away before the first breath of the breeze and leave nothing behind? Nothing to lay hold of. [67]

Willems's "vague, disgusting, and terrible" actions violate not only a simple, conventional moral code of conduct (the initial theft, for example), but also a deeper convention, an ethical standard reflected in Lingard's naturalistic moral order. The old order – the "sea of the past" – that Lingard represents is under attack; or at least Lingard feels that this is so: he cannot quite see or understand his opponents because they are much like "a band of assassins in the darkness of vast and unsafe places." How can he fight those who merely "hover" and lurk around him? In an ironic deployment of the expression, Lingard can see "right through Willems" to nothing that would account for the betrayal; Lingard's "prolonged glance" leads to an indecipherable, possibly insubstantial truth – an "unsteady mist" that might "leave nothing behind."

Lingard registers Nietzsche's Hamlet who realizes the Dionysian truth of a chaotic universe beneath an illusion of order. The crisis is replete with pathos, but the narrator also makes us see that it is temporary and opens onto genuinely philosophical recognition, which must pass through an experience of perplexity, unknowing, or wonder.[68] Willems inadvertently forces Lingard to confront that "misty," potentially treacherous, aspect of human nature that defies reason: "The thing could not be explained. An unexampled, cold-blooded treachery, awful, incomprehensible. Why did he do it? Why? The old seaman in the stuffy solitude of his little cabin on board the schooner groaned out many times that question, striking with an open palm his perplexed forehead."[69] The captain wonders why Willems should have so badly betrayed a man who had, like a father, provided for him. The narrator's description of the "stuffy solitude" within which Lingard is thinking suggests that his moral framework may be too rigid: it leaves no room for "cold-blooded" and "incomprehensible" treachery. Ironically, then, Willems inadvertently forces Lingard beyond his "little cabin." The captain's "perplex[ity]" speaks to Aristotle's claim that philosophy begins with puzzlement or wonder: Lingard is on the threshold of a genuine experience of recognition as a return to, or recovery of, the truth.

Lingard might have found solace in the thought that "the thing could not be explained" – but it is not in his nature to stop at mere indeterminacy. The captain eventually finds his bearings: "Who could suspect, who could guess, who could imagine what's in you? I couldn't! You are my mistake. I shall hide you here [...] Do not expect me to forgive you [...] To me you are not Willems, the man I befriended, and helped through thick and thin and thought much of...You are not a human being that may be destroyed or forgiven. You are a bitter thought, a something without a body and that must be hidden...You are my shame."[70] In a classical moment of recognition, Lingard admits his error in judgment and voices his shame. His decision to abandon rather than "destroy" Willems suggests that Lingard has learned something: acting between extremes of forgiveness and destruction, he exercises moderate compassion; he shows no sign of the sentimentality that led to his downfall. Nietzsche might argue that Lingard's shame indicates a concern for reputation that taints or calls into question his nobility and sense of justice, and that Lingard's decision to keep Willems "hidden" amounts to a denial rather than a truly courageous confrontation with the truth. Indeed, a modern reader might prefer that Lingard integrate the darkness, the shadow, into his worldview. But Lingard's rejection of his protégé implies that we are morally responsible for upholding an understanding and expectation of human possibilities against Willems's utterly debased condition.

An Outcast of the Islands does not finally vindicate modern pathos. Captain Lingard embodies a form of moral excellence that Conrad clearly wants us to recognize and celebrate in contrast to the Willemses of the world. Between the compassionate, formidable Lingard and the sceptical unnamed narrator, Conrad is beginning to formulate a narrator who might offer an outlook on nature and human nature as subject to chance, risk, and accident, without assuming that any amount of "incertitude" or failure to see renders illusory every claim to knowledge, including judgments of character and conduct. However, to fully appreciate *An Outcast* as a formative moment in Conrad's literary response to modern extremes, we must turn to Conrad's masterpiece, *Lord Jim: A Tale*.

3

Seeing Jim's Virtues in *Lord Jim: A Tale*

The conquest of love, honour, men's confidence – the pride of it, the power of it, are fit materials for a heroic tale; only our minds are struck by the externals of such a success, and to Jim's successes there were no externals. Thirty miles of forest shut it off from the sight of an indifferent world, and the noise of the white surf along the coast over-powered the voice of fame.[1]

But do you notice how, three hundred miles beyond the end of telegraph cables and mail-boat lines, the haggard utilitarian lies of our civilization wither and die, to be replaced by pure exercises of imagination, that have the futility, often the charm and sometimes the deep hidden truthfulness, of works of art?[2]

An Outcast of the Islands is a formative moment in Conrad's literary career. As Aristotle's theory of tragedy helps us recognize, a moderate outlook on character and conduct begins to emerge in the novel between Lingard's compassion and the unnamed narrator's rational, sceptical distance from the action. *An Outcast*'s unnamed narrator makes us see that even if Lingard and "the old sea" are disappearing into a sphere of action governed by extremes, Lingard's classically tragic character provides us with a point of reference for appreciating the deeper significance of "the sea of today," including and especially Peter Willems's excessive investment in the individual will as a paradoxical symptom of modern pathos. The artistic and philosophical implications of narrative perspective in *An Outcast* become even more apparent, however, when they are considered with Charlie Marlow, Conrad's compassionate yet sceptical character-narrator *par excellence* – particularly as he appears in one of Conrad's most celebrated and tragic novels, *Lord Jim: A Tale* (1900).[3]

As many critics have pointed out, character-narrator Charlie Marlow is not Conrad. And yet, Conrad describes Marlow in such intimate terms that we cannot deny that their voices and outlooks are sympathetic – that, as Aristotle would say, Marlow is to Conrad "another self."[4] In an Author's Note published five years after Marlow's final appearance, Conrad writes of Marlow in terms of friendship: "he haunts my hours of solitude, when, in silence, we lay our heads together in great comfort and harmony" and that "of all my people [Marlow is] the one that has never been a vexation to my spirit. A most discreet understanding man."[5] Indeed, Marlow's discretion and understanding – in harmony, Conrad suggests, with his own temperament – are increasingly apparent in the four novels where he appears. In "Youth: A Narrative" (1898) and *Heart of Darkness* (1899) Marlow relates the events of his own remarkable experiences – his original voyage into the East, and his passage up the Congo river respectively. In *Lord Jim* and *Chance: A Tale in Two Parts* (which Conrad began in 1905 and completed until 1912) we see Marlow's sustained attention shift to the eventful lives of others.

Lord Jim focuses on Marlow's searching narrative about his friendship with the title character – a young, disgraced sailor whom he befriends in Bombay (Mumbai) during a public inquiry known as "the *Patna* affair." Marlow's listeners – one of whom is the novel's opening frame narrator – would have heard of Jim, the first mate of the *Patna* who joined the skipper and the ship's second engineer in abandoning the ship and her 800 Mecca-bound passengers in an apparent crisis. At the time, the crew is certain that their rusty old steamer was bound to sink after having "collided with something floating awash."[6] However, after being rescued by a British ship and brought to Bombay, they learn that a French gunboat discovered the stricken *Patna* and towed her ashore to Aden (city of Yemen). In his private testimony over dinner with Marlow, Jim's defensive insistence that he is different from and morally superior to the dishonourable members of his crew appears to have some truth: he is the only one courageous enough to endure the inquiry, including the humiliating cancellation of his seaman's certificate. What truly compels Marlow, however, is the intensity of Jim's anguished account of his experience, the youth's almost irremediable suffering at the loss, not so much of his certification, but of his sense of honour.

Recalling Lingard's efforts to help Willems in the aftermath of the young clerk's initial transgression, Marlow intervenes – pragmatically at first, by finding Jim work as a means of physical survival. Still, Jim's moral suffering prevents him from making use of Marlow's help: the youth cannot stay with any job because stories about the *Patna* incident seem to have spread everywhere, so that he feels relentlessly pursued by his dishonourable past.[7] Marlow then turns for advice to his longtime, sympathetic friend Stein. Seeking to relieve Jim of his unrelenting self-judgment, Marlow and Stein decide to send him to work as a trading clerk in Patusan, a little-known district on an island so removed from an increasingly interconnected world of "telegraph cables and mail-boat lines" that Jim can escape the gossip about the *Patna* affair.

Aristotle gives us a framework and a language with which to see Jim – with Marlow – as higher and nobler than many of his critics allow, and as a figure who reflects Conrad's deeply sceptical outlook on the possibilities of genuine agency in the modern world.[8] Jim has been criticized as an embodiment of romantic egotism, as a "'beautiful soul' who values his purity and his romantic self-image, above all worldly entanglements and imperfections."[9] And yet, even critics such as John Lester and Lee Horsley – both of whom describe Jim as a "romantic egoist" – acknowledge the inadequacy of this description when they note Jim's heroic sense of justice in the aristocratic culture of Patusan.[10] As Gerald Garmon remarks, "such egoism has always been one of the most salient characteristics of the hero."[11] Aristotle helps us see that Jim's sense of justice can be realized only in an ancient, potentially tragic sphere of action which the novel juxtaposes with the *Patna*, a fleshed-out representation of *An Outcast*'s "sea of to-day." Taken together, *An Outcast of the Islands* and *Lord Jim* imply that classically tragic figures such as Lingard and Jim give us perspective on modernity because they are anachronistic. The difference is that Lingard exists on the margins of *An Outcast*, whereas Jim is the central, title character and he is young – details that suggest Conrad's need to celebrate examples of ancient virtue even or especially when they appear to be increasingly unlikely.

"The *Patna* Affair" and Modern Pathos

Literary critic A.C. Bradley's essay on Hegel's philosophical definition of tragic conflict illuminates Hegel and Aristotle's shared preoccupation with action.[12] As we saw in the previous chapter, Aristotle calls tragic error "hamartia," a term that invokes archery and the doctrine of the mean: tragic figures fall when they act and "miss the mark" between extremes.[13] Hegel's formulation follows a similar logic: tragedy occurs when one encounters a collision between two equally justified "goods"; the hero falls when pushing one good too far. Bradley explains:

> In many a work of art, in many a statue, picture, tale, or song, such powers are shown in solitary peace or harmonious co-operation. Tragedy shows them in collision. Their nature is divine, and in religion they appear as gods; but, as seen in the world of tragic action, they have left the repose of

Olympus, have entered into human wills, and now meet as foes. And this spectacle if sublime is also terrible. The essentially tragic fact is the self-division and intestinal warfare of the ethical substance, not so much the war of good with evil as the war of good with good. Two of these isolated powers face each other, making incompatible demands. The family claims what the state refuses, love requires what honor forbids. The competing forces are in themselves rightful, and so far the claim of each is equally justified; but the right of each is pushed into a wrong, because it ignores the right of the other, and demands that absolute sway which belongs to neither alone, but to the whole of which each is but a part.

And one reason why this happens lies in the nature of the characters through whom these claims are made. It is the nature of the tragic hero, at once his greatness and his doom, that he knows no shrinking or half-heartedness, but identifies himself wholly with the power that moves him, and will admit the justification of no other power.[14]

Bradley contrasts art that represents goods, powers, or forces in cooperation or equilibrium with works of tragedy where such equally justified powers or forces collide. In a one-sided action, the tragic figure pushes one good or power so far that it eclipses the other, causing the hero to fall. As the *Poetics* teaches, in working through "a serious, complete action [i.e., conflict] which has magnitude," tragedy shows just how heroic it is to sustain competing demands in equilibrium.[15] In witnessing the tragic figure's fall, we feel pity (judging that the hero suffers more than she deserves) and terror (by recognizing ourselves, our own possibilities, in the hero's flawed humanity). Hegel's dialectical outlook on the tragic is uplifting – for the "ethical substance" reasserts itself by way of a human intervention.[16] Aristotle, too, integrates the restorative, elevating nature of tragedy into his formulation by way of catharsis.[17] As the *Poetics* and Book VIII of the *Politics* explain, the audience of citizens return to the *polis* with a clarified understanding of the virtues and their relationship to human flourishing or happiness.

Conrad carefully structures *Lord Jim* to make us see that on the steamer, Jim does not experience a classically tragic collision between two goods, but a collision as murky and unknowable as the mysterious object that hits the steamship. Jim is not and could not be heroic or even tragically heroic under such circumstances, but merely pathetic.[18] The first section of the novel contains three crises: An initial, minor crisis occurs aboard a training ship; a second crisis occurs during Jim's early, untested career as "chief mate of a fine ship"; and a third, central crisis takes place aboard the *Patna*, "a local steamer as old as the hills."[19] The first two events anticipate the *Patna* as properly pathetic, where the key event is inherently indeterminate – complicating any final or certain judgment about Jim's conduct there.

The frame narrator's opening account of Jim's experience on a training ship invites us to consider that we ourselves as readers are being trained to see – to take in, and distinguish between – all the details. For example, Jim has "a steady head" and is "very smart aloft," where, at his literal and symbolic station above his peers in the "fore-top," he gazes with pleasure at "the hazy splendour of the sea in the distance and the hope of a stirring life in the world of adventure."[20] Jim's literally lofty position may hint at irony; however, the narrator soon suggests that Jim's belief that he is different might contain some merit, some truth: "on the lower deck in the babel of two hundred voices he would forget himself, and beforehand live in his mind the sea-life of light literature. He saw himself saving people from sinking ships, cutting away masts in a hurricane, swimming through a surf with a line; [...] – always an example of devotion to duty and as unflinching as a hero in a book."[21] As an inexperienced sailor-in-training, Jim knows only romantic depictions of heroism from books; the narrator later points out that his ideals remain untested. Still, the narrator also suggests that Jim's spirited imagination and longing for adventure set him apart from those who belong to "the babel of two hundred voices." Ironically, Jim's dreams of heroism are more substantial than those of most young sailors who are much like the storied, ordinary workmen in the Old Testament who foolishly imagine they can build a tower to reach the heavens. If Jim recalls what we saw in the previous chapter of Peter Willems's sense of grandeur, the frame narrator of *Lord Jim* exhibits none of the harsh mockery that we find in *An Outcast*'s opening description of its protagonist. Instead, there is a restrained yet knowingly ironic perspective – an understanding of youthful spiritedness untouched by experience.

Just as Conrad's frame narrator prepares readers to distinguish Jim from his peers, the training ship episode teaches us – as spectators on Jim's experience – to consider circumstances when appraising character. Jim luxuriates in watching "the big ships departing, the broad-beamed ferries constantly on the move" and "the little boats floating far below his feet." This peaceful setting is displaced by "threatening glimpses of the tumbling tide, [...] the broad ferry-boats pitching ponderously at anchor."[22] When a "coaster" ship collides with "a schooner at anchor" the instructor and students lower a boat to rescue the sailors. Jim, surprised by the fury of the storm, misses his chance to join the mission, and another boy gets to act the hero.[23] Although initially upset at what appeared to be a missed opportunity, upon reflection Jim concludes that "he could affront greater perils [than the gale]. He would do so – better than anybody."[24] The narrative's free indirect discourse could be an ironic comment on Jim's attempt to rationalize his failure. Then again, the boy who intervened confirms Jim's perspective on the crisis:

> "I just saw his head bobbing and I dashed my boat-hook in the water. It caught in his breeches and I nearly went overboard, as I thought I would, only old Symons let go the tiller and grabbed my legs – the boat nearly swamped. Old Symons is a fine old chap. I don't mind a bit him being grumpy with us. He swore at me all the time he held my leg, but that was only his way of telling me to stick to the boat-hook. Old Symons is awfully excitable – isn't he? No – not the little fair chap – the other, the big one with a beard. When we pulled him in he groaned 'Oh, my leg! oh, my leg!' and turned up his eyes. Fancy such a big chap fainting like a girl. Would any of you fellows faint for a jab with a boat-hook? – I wouldn't. It went into his leg so far." He showed the boat-hook, which he had carried below for the purpose, and produced a sensation. "No, silly! It was not his flesh that held him – his breeches did. Lots of blood, of course."[25]

The boy avidly mocks those who would believe they had been in any real danger during the rescue. He laughs at "Old Symons," the training ship's captain whose "excitable" temperament caused him to overreact to the event, and mocks the wounded man who fainted at the mere appearance of a serious injury (there was "lots of blood"), even though it was only the result of "a jab with a boat-hook." Moreover, the would-be hero mocks one of his listeners, a fellow student – "No, silly! It was not his flesh that held him – his breeches did." Reinforcing this comical outlook on events is the narrator's affectionately satirical description of the "sensation" that the sight of the boathook creates among the students.

The satirical remark, combined with the boy's account of the accident, supports Jim's conclusion that he needn't regret his inaction. It gives weight to Jim's reflection that "he was rather glad he had not gone into the cutter since a lower achievement had served the turn. He had enlarged his knowledge more than those who had done the work."[26] The "knowledge" that Jim gains is that courage and cowardice are not simply defined by fight or flight, but rather depend on a clear-eyed assessment of the situation: "Unnoticed and apart from the noisy crowd of boys, he exulted with fresh certitude in his avidity for adventure and in a sense of many-sided courage."[27] His thinking cannot, given the details, be simply taken as an egotistical rationalization. Such an extreme view would jar with the text – the details of what actually transpired on the ship, the truth of Jim's insight. We can see Jim even more clearly against the example of his predecessor, *An Outcast*'s Peter Willems.[28] Jim's attempt to restore his sense of self lacks Willems's cruel and overtly deluded grandiosity; instead of cutting irony, in *Lord Jim*'s frame narrator we hear a rational, almost objective voice that would leave it to us to recognize the substance of Jim's insight.

Aristotle's *Nicomachean Ethics* can shed light on what Jim learns – that fear and inaction in and of themselves are not always or necessarily a sign of cowardice:

> a courageous man could be said to be someone who is fearless when it comes to a noble death and to any situation that brings death suddenly to hand. What pertains to war is above all of this character. Yet surely the courageous man is fearless also at sea and in sicknesses, though not in the way that sailors are. For the courageous man despairs of his preservation and is disgusted with this sort of death, whereas the sailors are of good hope, given their experience. But at the same time too, the courageous act like men in circumstances where prowess in battle is possible or dying is noble; but in the sorts of destruction mentioned, by contrast, neither such prowess nor nobility is possible.[29]

The courageous man may be said to be "fearless" in general – whether he faces dying in an act of heroism, a "noble death," or by another cause. However, his fearlessness is complicated by a higher kind of fear – of a purposeless death, by mere accident or illness. The courageous man wants more than mere survival and is unimpressed by the chance to simply follow the rules. He is mostly repulsed (or "disgusted") by death in sickness or shipwreck, situations that would render him passive or pathetic. Aristotle helps us see that the gale paralyses Jim not because he is afraid of dying, but because he was "tak[en] unawares" by the sudden onset of the storm. Jim's instructor sees this lack of readiness when he kindly advises that the event "will teach [Jim] to be smart."[30] The comment is ironic: as it turns out, the rescue is not in fact, as Aristotle puts it, "a situation that brings death suddenly to hand"; as a result, it would have been "smart" or prudent, anyway, to intentionally hang back and let someone else intervene. Later, Marlow distinguishes between this admirable desire and what might appear to be a kind of egotism or selfishness: "Jim's selfishness had a higher origin, a more lofty aim."[31]

Preparing us for the *Patna* collision where Jim faces "the sorts of destruction" that preclude an exercise of "prowess" and "nobility," the frame narrator relates the details of a second crisis when Jim is exposed to the darker realities of nature at his first post as a "chief mate of a fine ship."[32] During a severe storm Jim gets a "glimpse of" a "truth [which] is not so often made apparent as people might think [...] [nature's seemingly] sinister violence of intention – that indefinable something which forces it upon the mind and the heart of a man, that this complication of accidents or these elemental furies are coming at him [...] to smash, to destroy, to annihilate all he had seen, known, loved, enjoyed or hated; all that is priceless and necessary – the sunshine, the memories, the future – which means to sweep the whole precious world utterly away from his sight by the simple and appalling act of taking his life."[33] The narrator refers to "man" rather than sailors in particular – universalizing this terrifying experience of complete subjugation to nature – a stark reminder of the limits of our considerable capacity for agency. When nature "forces" its seeming "violence of intention" on the "mind and heart of a man" it renders him painfully aware of his mortality. In fact, Jim is rendered doubly passive: after having been "injured by a falling spar" he is confined to his cabin, "dazed, battered, hopeless and tormented as if at the bottom of an abyss of unrest."[34] In his anguish Jim relinquishes his love of heroism – his spirited intention to die, if he must die, a noble death: he "did not care what the end would be." The narrator qualifies this feeling, though, commenting that "in his lucid moments [Jim] overvalued his indifference."[35] Jim responds to the revealed truth of nature's annihilative potential and the bare fact of his own mortality with "indifference" towards his "end." Nevertheless, the narrator explains that "the danger [of the real of nature], when not seen, has the imperfect vagueness of human thought. The fear grows shadowy; and Imagination, the enemy of men, the father of all terrors, unstimulated, sinks to rest in the dullness of exhausted emotion."[36] In this brilliant inversion, the narrator tells us that Jim's "indifference" – a pathetic sense of emptiness or meaninglessness – is the illusion, here. If he were not stuck below in his cabin, Jim would "care what the end would be." Not directly witnessing the reality, the imagination fades. If the imagination is "the enemy of men" it is not necessarily false, because it can ironically indicate or facilitate an active or true participation in reality. This situation – where Jim has at least on the surface given up on his heroic aspirations – prepares us for the third, central crisis at sea.

At the outset of *Lord Jim* Conrad is careful to include details in the frame narrator's account that point to the *Patna* as a prime example of pathos.[37] Having been stalled in hospital "at an Eastern port,"[38] Jim meets other sailors in town who had also been "thrown there by some accident." These men "now had a horror of home service with its harder conditions, severer view of duty and the hazard of storm oceans [...]"

and in all they said – in their actions, in their looks, in their persons –
could be detected the soft spot, the place of decay, the determination to
lounge safely through existence."[39] And so, Jim is surrounded by men
who sharply contrast with what we have seen of Jim's spirited longing
for those real life-and-death situations where he might courageously
intervene. The narrator explains that in this environment Jim is at first
disdainful of the appearance of an easy life, and then sees its appeal –
having "found a fascination in the sight of those men, in their appearance of doing so well on such a small allowance of danger and toil."[40]
Charmed, even mesmerized, by images of an apparently easy life, Jim
gives up on going home – "suddenly" or arbitrarily taking a position
of chief mate on a "derelict," rust-eaten Mecca-bound steamship.[41] He
falls into the position.

If the frame narrator guides us to associate the *Patna* with arbitrari-
ness and passivity, his description of the seemingly peaceful conditions
at sea aboard the steamer echoes the state of equilibrium that makes up
the ethical substance of ancient tragedy, only to differentiate the *Patna*
from the (potentially tragic) hero's context:

> A marvelous stillness pervaded the world, and the stars, together with
> the serenity of their rays, seemed to shed upon the earth the assurance of
> everlasting security [...] The propeller turned without a check as though its
> beat had been part of the scheme of a safe universe [...]
>
>   Jim on the bridge was penetrated by the great certitude of unbounded
> safety and peace that could be read on the silent aspect of nature like the
> certitude of fostering love upon a mother's face.[42]

The narrator compares Jim's experience to an originary symbiosis
between mother and child. Just as the mother's calm, loving gaze
becomes the infant's mirror, the placid sea becomes a mirror for Jim's
fantasies of heroism: "At such times his thoughts would be full of valor-
ous deeds; [...] they passed before him with a heroic tread; they carried
his soul away with them and made it drunk with the divine philtre of
an unbounded confidence in itself."[43] The narrator later implies that this
intoxication is much like a return to infancy, the "pleasurable languor
running through [Jim's] every limb as though all the blood in his body
had turned to warm milk."[44] As the narrator's words "seemed" and "as
though" indicate, the promise of "everlasting security" is both a memory and an impossible ideal. Unlike the substance of tragically heroic
action, where there is an achieved state of equilibrium between two
goods – again, what Aristotle describes as those natural familial relationships that should be harmonious but conflict in tragic poetry – the

harmony or unity aboard the *Patna* are illusory.[45] In this blissful state, Jim's mistake is to forget the terrible reality that he glimpsed at his previous post: Nature is ripe with chance or accident and, unlike the "unattainable" with which Jim seems so "hungrily preoccupied," human nature is equally imperfect.[46] There is no actual state of equilibrium here, only the pathos of prelapsarian illusion.

The collision itself underlines the pathos of the *Patna* affair – for it was barely perceptible, much like "a snake crawling over a stick,"[47] as Jim explains during the official inquiry into the affair. The narrator's remark that the comparison is "apt" draws our attention to the ominous allusion to the inevitable fall; added to this is the abyssal horror (the truth is that there is no truth) of the whole experience, which is so different from the justice-oriented emotion of terror in ancient tragedy. The narrator remarks that Jim realizes "only a meticulous precision of statement would bring out the true horror behind the appalling face of things."[48] On the "face of things," the captain and crew of the *Patna* abandoned a ship with 800 passengers: a perfectly detailed recollection of the event would "bring out" the awful, murky indeterminacy of it all.

Jim's factual testimony and the private testimony of the French officer whose gunboat, *The Avondale*, towed the *Patna* ashore, certainly contain details that would unsettle the assessors' conclusions about Jim's conduct. For example, Jim reports that his initial response to the collision was calm and dutiful. He followed the captain's orders, which were to go below deck to investigate while "mak[ing] no noise for fear of creating a panic" – a "precaution" that Jim found "reasonable."[49] The soundness of this decision became even clearer when Jim saw the extent of the damage and decided, with his colleagues, that the already-precarious steamer was on the verge of sinking. Marlow urges his listeners to see that Jim responsibly followed orders, and that his assessment of the ship was fair enough. He claims that "any other man in [Jim's] place" would have believed "that the ship would go down at any moment."[50] Reinforcing this perspective is Marlow's interview with the French officer who recalls that he "had advised his commander that the safest thing to do was to leave [the bulkhead] alone, it was so villainous to look at" and "demanded the greatest care (*exigeait les plus grands ménagements*)."[51] Thus Jim was understandably certain that the ship was going to sink – especially given the approaching storm – and under those conditions remained admirably calm in an apparent emergency. He refused to join the crew's "antics in which they displayed their extreme aversion to die" – their struggle to release a boat so that they could save their own lives.[52] Instead, he "cut the life boats clear of the ship," hoping to save at least some passengers. Jim was consumed by the dreadful fact that there were only seven boats for eight hundred passengers.

In other words, Jim was trapped in an impossible dilemma. Marlow compares it to "low comedy" with "an element of burlesque in his ordeal – a degradation of funny grimaces in the approach of death or dishonor."[53] This comparison amplifies the distance between Jim's situation aboard the *Patna* and ancient tragedy: instead of being caught between two goods, Jim found himself absurdly caught between death – not, it should be noted, the possibility of an *honourable* death – and dishonour.[54] While Jim inwardly willed the ship to "Sink – curse you! Sink!," the captain and first and second engineers clumsily struggled to release a boat so they might save their own lives.[55] Marlow describes Jim's recollection of the degrading scene: the desperate men "would fall back before it time after time, stand swearing at each other, and suddenly make another rush in a bunch ... 'Enough to make you die laughing,' he commented with downcast eyes; then raising them for a moment to my face with a dismal smile, 'I ought to have a merry life of it, by God! for I shall see that funny sight a good many times yet before I die.'"[56] This kind of comedy is not ancient tragedy's elevating counterpart, but is, to use Marlow's word again, "degrading" – evoking only bitter laughter. As Marlow implies with the word "burlesque" – which he repeats in reflecting on "the burlesque meanness pervading that particular disaster" – the whole affair is a mere mockery of a crisis at sea.[57]

Thus Marlow uses the phrase "passive heroism" to describe Jim's initial refusal to participate in the other crew members' desertion of the *Patna*.[58] To qualify "heroism" with "passive" could mean that Jim was not truly or fully heroic – but it also suggests that there was room only for a qualified version of heroism under such circumstances, where Jim and the crew, reasonably enough, believed that the ship was doomed. Marlow gently mocks Jim's youthful idealism – explaining that when Jim realized "he could do nothing," he "stiffened in the idea of some sort of heroic discretion"[59] – in the idea, that is, of stoically going down with the ship. Marlow sees the futility in such an attitude since Jim ended up abandoning ship anyway; but the prospective act itself seemed futile. Even the French officer of the *Avondale* explains that when he discovered the *Patna* it was only "after ascertaining through his binoculars that the crowd on deck did not look plague-stricken [that he] decided to send a boat."[60] They were prepared to cut loose the steamer: "all the time of towing we had two quartermasters stationed with axes by the hawsers, to cut us clear of our tow in case she..."[61] This is not a shameful admission: the French officer claims that he cannot comment on lost honour because he knows nothing about it. In other words, taking action to avoid unnecessary death is not necessarily a moral failure; it all depends on the details of the situation, and on the agent's intentions. Conrad makes us see the episode with compassion for Jim, and he (perhaps paradoxically) appeals to our capacity for reason by giving us an example of modern pathos – where our judgments are interminably qualified by the details because the conditions themselves are indeterminate.

Patusan and Ancient Tragedy

Aristotle's theory of tragedy illuminates the novel's two major, contrasting settings and actions on the *Patna* (including the arrival of an ambiguous, destructive element), and the remote island of Patusan where Marlow, with his friend Stein, transport Jim in an effort to help him. In Patusan – so different from the *Patna*'s world – Jim finds an ancient sphere of action where he becomes a tragic hero who pushes his admirable love of honour too far, causing him to lose the balance he has achieved there, between his public and private lives.

Visiting Jim nearly two years after his departure for the island, Marlow observes what appears to be a relation of peaceful reciprocity between Jim and the community – an example of the equilibrium to which Bradley refers, which is also the condition of human flourishing. Marlow comments on his friend's newfound happiness: "He looked with an owner's eye at the peace of the evening, at the river, at the houses, at the everlasting life of the forests, at the life of the old mankind, at the secrets of the land, at the pride of his own heart; but it was they that possessed him and made him their own to the innermost thought, to the slightest stir of blood, to his last breath."[62] This reference to nature's immutability, to "the everlasting life of the forests," recalls the frame narrator's description of the calm before the *Patna* collision. This time, however, we have none of the narrator's qualifying words such as "seemed" or "as though." To be sure, at this point in his story Marlow has not yet received news of Jim's death, whereas – as we saw – the frame narrator describes Jim's blissful state aboard the *Patna* retrospectively, thus in full knowledge of what is to come. Even so, the illusory quality of the "marvelous stillness" aboard the ship in the frame narrator's account has less to do with its impermanence (fine weather is real, even though it is temporary) and more to do with how that peaceful state enables Jim to indulge in fantasy and forget the chance-ridden nature of nature. By contrast, Marlow describes an achieved, concrete beauty rather than what we saw of Jim's pre-lapsarian illusion of everlasting peace and harmony with nature.[63] On the island Jim ostensibly rules as "Tuan Jim": Jim is both "owner" and "owned," rendering his people both owners and owned as well – and Patusan is "the land he was destined to fill with the fame of his virtues," especially his love of honour.[64] Jim can truly feel at peace there because he has earned it; when he gazes at his community in "the peace of the evening" he sees a reflection not of dreams and fantasies, but of his capacity to hit the mark of right action in extraordinary circumstances. If Jim still worries about whether he has been "fair to all parties," this concern is a mark of his genuine nobility.[65] The people look to him a figure who maintains justice by mediating even the obscurest disputes.

In Patusan, Jim heroically achieves a harmonious state between public honour on the one hand, and private friendship and love on the other, that his title – "Lord Jim," given to him by the local aristocratic Malaysian people, the "Bugis" – reflects. The island is in chaos when Jim arrives – confirming Marlow's friend Stein's prediction: "as far as [Stein] was aware (the last news were thirteen months old he stated precisely), utter insecurity for life and property was the normal condition."[66] Two warring factions, led by Rajah Tunku Allang on the one hand and the rogue leader Sherif Ali on the other, are exploiting Bugis leader Doramin and his people. There are ongoing, weekly "faction fights" over trade between Rajah Allang and Doramin: "Villages were burnt, men were dragged into the Rajah's stockade to be killed or tortured for the crime of trading with anybody else but himself."[67] Marlow describes the perpetual violence on the island: "There wasn't a week without some fight in Patusan at that time," explaining that "only a day or two before Jim's arrival several heads of households in the very fishing village that was afterwards taken under his especial protection had been driven over the cliffs by a party of the Rajah's spearmen, on suspicion of having been collecting edible birds' nests for a Celebes trader."[68] If Doramin and Rajah Allang are at war over trade, Sherif Ali prevents them from negotiating an agreement by recruiting "tribes in the interior" to attack both sides – keeping everyone helpless. In short, Jim facilitates peace and stability in Patusan by launching and winning a war against the third party who has been terrorizing Doramin and Rajah Allang's communities.[69] Sherif Ali ends up leaving the country – and Rajah Allang is chastened by the Bugis's victory against such a formidable opponent. As a result of the war, Doramin can once again hope that Dain will succeed him as the rightful indigenous ruler of Patusan.

Jim hits the mark between public honour and what the novel suggests is an equally justified but private good – what Marlow calls "the individual side of the story" – in his romance with a girl he affectionately calls "Jewel." It may seem objectionable that Jim names Jewel, and yet Jim is himself named by the Bugis. Thus naming appears in the novel as an act of honouring the other rather than a straightforward exertion of power.[70] Marlow learns that Jim helped Jewel escape her stepfather Cornelius, the abusive and "fundamentally and outwardly abject" agent whom Stein sent Jim to replace.[71] However, the rescue complicates what might on the surface appear to be conventional, paternalistic exercise of colonial power typical of mere romance: "It wasn't that he pitied her so much, he affirmed; it was more than pity; it was as if he had something on his conscience, while that life went on."[72] Jim's remark ranks the moral emotions – situating pity below true love, a private emotion infused with a sense of justice that is also reflected in Jim's breathless, preciously unguarded expression of respect for the girl: "can't tell you how much I owe to her – and so – you understand – I – exactly as if."[73] Reciprocity defines their private relationship, mirroring Jim's public relationship with the community where, again, he "look[s] with an owner's eye" on the landscape and the village while "it was they that possessed him and made him their own to the innermost thought."[74] Marlow's use of the article "the" gives his comment a mysterious, philosophical depth. But his point seems to be to mark for his listeners the limits of his account: he wants to preserve the otherness of the other – or perhaps the Bugis's ownership of Jim blurs the boundary between public or political and private, in contrast with modern conventions. In any case, Jim's happiness is a remarkable achievement – a balance between competing elements of honour and love that dramatizes the conditions of ancient tragedy.

Marlow's account of Jim's life in Patusan emphasizes the wonder of Jim's success in a sphere of action that is geographically and intrinsically different from the modern West. As Michael Valdez Moses explains in his reading of *Lord Jim* as a post-historical novel, in Patusan "fundamental political issues are not settled" – an expression of Conrad's "concerns about [the homogenizing] effects of modernization."[75] For example, Marlow points out that "without the weight of Doramin's authority and his son's fiery enthusiasm, [Jim] would have failed."[76] Jim's mode of leadership is cooperative – a detail that complicates the colonialist binary of colonizer and colonized, oppressor and oppressed, just as it challenges the apparent, generic conventions of Jim's story. Moreover, while one might view the story as a typical tale of courage – of "prowess in battle," as Aristotle would say – Marlow sees finer or deeper virtues in Jim's actions: "It was not so much of his fearlessness that I thought. It was strange how little account I took of it: as if it had been something too conventional to be at the root of the matter. No. I was more struck by the other gifts he had displayed. He had proved his grasp of the unfamiliar situation, his intellectual alertness in that field of thought. There was his readiness too! Amazing."[77] In a remark that recalls what Jim himself learned aboard the training ship – that courage is a "many-sided virtue" – Marlow implies that Jim's achievements in Patusan diminish his previous disgrace. He focuses on how Jim handled an entirely "unfamiliar situation"– a context that demanded the more interesting, because finer, virtues of "intellectual alertness" and a "readiness" to act. Marlow clearly ranks these virtues – including the capacity to discern what is needed – as higher or deeper than "fearlessness," which he views as too ordinary or "conventional" compared to the qualities of character on which courage relies.

Despite his readiness and alertness, however, Jim fails – following the trajectory of the classical tragic hero who misses the mark between competing or equally justified claims on his loyalty. Jewel senses the impermanence of their happiness, "guard[ing] her conquest inflexibly – as though he were hard to keep."[78] She intuits that Jim values honour more than love – that he lives for what Marlow calls a "shadowy ideal" rather than the real, flesh-and-blood woman before him.[79] The details of Jim's error in judgment are in Marlow's letter to "the privileged reader" – one of Marlow's listeners – for whom Marlow gathers fragments of information from conversations with Stein, Jewel, and Jim's friend, the Bugis trader Tamb' Itam, and the misanthropic Gentleman Brown.[80] He writes that Brown arrives at Patusan with his crew of fourteen starving men while Jim is away in the interior. Brown is especially dangerous among his storied peers "for the arrogant temper of his misdeeds and a vehement scorn for mankind at large and for his victims in particular [...] He would rob a man as if only to demonstrate his poor opinion of the creature."[81] As it happens, one of the Rajah's diplomats, Kassim, sees Brown's arrival in Jim's absence as a chance to finally end Jim's rule. Kassim facilitates an alliance between Cornelius and Brown so that both of them might be used to destroy Jim and his Bugis followers. In the meantime, Brown promises to cooperate with Kassim in exchange for food, while privately making plans to join forces with Jim instead, whom Brown cynically presumes will agree to exploit the island. Brown realizes that Jim does "not look like a man who would be willing to give anything for assistance," and persuades Jim to give his crew passage with their weapons.[82]

Jim embodies what the ancient Greeks knew so well – that heroes risk identifying themselves so strongly with one good, such as the public good that motivates them, that they annihilate the claims of life and love. Recalling Lingard's straightforward generosity with Willems, Jim expects that his honesty and sense of justice will compel an honest and just response. His lordly offer to Brown – "You shall have a clear road or else a clear fight"[83] – ominously echoes Jim's description of his experience aboard the *Patna*, that it "was not like a fight,"[84] signalling Brown as yet another object with which Jim's "ship" collides, while the repetition makes us differentiate the two events.

As we have seen, Marlow makes it very clear that *Patna* crisis in all its ambiguity would have been overwhelming for even the most experienced seaman. In Patusan, however, Jim is truly at fault: believing that he is invincible, he underestimates the threat that Brown and Cornelius pose because he pushes his love of honour too far. We see this danger when Jim reflects on the *Patna* in Patusan: "the bally thing," he remarks to Marlow, remains "at the back of [his] head."[85] Jim's inability to accept his flawed humanity leaves him susceptible to what Marlow describes as Brown's "subtle reference to their common blood, an assumption of common experience; a sickening suggestion of common guilt, of secret knowledge that was like a bond of their minds and of their hearts."[86] When Jim agrees to give Brown and his men passage, the lowly and resentful Cornelius works on Brown's vengeful pride by persuading him that Jim's response is insulting and deserves a reprisal. Cornelius leads Brown and his men to a narrow waterway on the other side of the island where they launch their surprise attack – what Marlow describes as "an act of cold-blooded ferocity" – on Dain Waris and others who have relaxed their watch, having received Jim's message that Brown and his men would leave peacefully.[87] Jim immediately understands that his community has lost trust in him – and so, despite Jewel's desperate plea that he run away with her, Jim presents himself to Chief Doramin for execution, a tragically elevating restoration of justice.

Echoing *An Outcast*, where we witness Lingard's forgiving response to Willems's first indiscretion in contrast with Willems's second, high-stakes betrayal, Marlow distinguishes between Jim's actions aboard the *Patna* on the one hand, and the events in Patusan on the other. Marlow explains that Jim "had retreated from one world, for a small matter of an impulsive jump, and now the other, the work of his own hands, had fallen in ruins upon his head,"[88] diminishing the importance of the *Patna* affair, a "small matter" of mere "impulse" rather than an intentional act. On the island, Jim's success and failure are profound – comprising (again) the "serious, complete action which has magnitude" that defines ancient tragedy in the *Poetics*.[89] Jim dies from Doramin's gunshot with "a proud and unflinching glance [...] with his hand over his lips."[90] The image reflects heroic resolve, a demonstration of virtue that is so complete it speaks for itself; it recalls

Hamlet's last words, implicitly positioning Jim as an admirable tragic figure in the tradition of Shakespeare and the ancient Greeks before him. In this case, however, no Fortinbras-figure arrives to take Dain's place – an absence that opens onto Conrad's historicist outlook on disappearing worlds in an increasingly homogeneous world. Jim's gesture also reflects his position at the enigmatic centre of Marlow's proliferating speech and writing, an expression of a mournful yearning for the old, increasingly elusive possibilities for heroic action.

Marlow's Narrative Heroism

The fact that Marlow addresses a group of men who would already be familiar with the *Patna* affair (even though, as Marlow remarks, he "is the only seaman here") in itself suggests that he is presenting a way of seeing that differs from the *status quo*.[91] Between the novel's fourth and seventeenth chapters, *Lord Jim* juxtaposes two modes of appraisal. At the outset we have the formal, public narrative of the courtroom and the official judgment of Jim's character that arises from that event – an official discourse which, although powerful in its public condemnation of Jim's conduct, seems ironically insignificant compared to the layered, nuanced oral and eventually epistolary narratives that take place beyond the limits of the courtroom. Marlow comments on the difference between the court's pragmatic interest in "the superficial how"[92] – restricted as they are by "proceedings ordained by law"[93] – and his own concern with both "the fundamental why" and "the state of a man's soul,"[94] situating himself and his listeners as an alternative, private group of assessors who might come to appraise Jim differently.[95] In other words, Marlow's alternative, truth-seeking narrative does not undermine appraisal of character in it itself. As Zdzisław Najder argues – challenging Douglas Hewitt's reading of the novel as a work about the impossibility of judgment – "the uncertainty of interpretation is only one element of the novel, not its essential message."[96] Indeed, Marlow's narrative is philosophical to the extent that it allows for what we cannot know without undermining knowledge and judgment altogether. As many critics have noted, the novel is as much about the truth as it is about the pursuit of it. Both Jim and Marlow want to get beyond the appearance of the *Patna* affair or crisis to its underlying truth and hence to the rightness or wrongness of Jim's conduct in it. Their pursuit of the truth suggests that truth-seeking itself is a heroic endeavour. And so, the frame narrator – again, one of Marlow's listeners – gives way to a character-narrator whose narrative we (along with Marlow's listeners) can ourselves witness in action, thus *as* itself an action.[97] Put differently,

Marlow-as-narrator performs a way of seeing, but he is also embedded in the action and thus simultaneously appeals to our ability to evaluate character – our ability, that is, to see his humanity and admire his excellence of character in action.

Marlow's distraction (by his own thoughts) from the sentence proceedings reflects the inadequacy of the assessors' conclusion that Jim, with the captain and engineers, acted "in utter disregard of their plain duty."[98] As James Phelan explains, "Marlow wants [...] to be as rigorous about and as responsible to the full evidence of Jim's life as possible" – that is, in a concerned, reflective, and determined pursuit of "evidence" that ironically exceeds the official language and the practical constraints of a courtroom inquiry.[99] Marlow meditates on the mysterious nature of the collision – especially given the court's conclusion that "there was no evidence to show the exact cause of the accident."[100] He draws his own conclusions, remarking that the object in question was a

> floating derelict, probably. I myself remember that a Norwegian barque bound out with a cargo of pitch-pine had been given up as missing about that time [...] a kind of maritime ghoul on the prowl to kill ships in the dark. Such wandering corpses are common enough in the North Atlantic, which is haunted by all the terrors of the sea – fogs, icebergs, dead ships bent upon mischief and long sinister gales that fasten upon one like a vampire till all the strength and the spirit and even hope are gone and one feels like the empty shell of a man. But there – in those seas – the incident was rare enough to resemble a special arrangement of a malevolent providence [...] an utterly aimless piece of devilry. This view occurring to me took off my attention.[101]

Marlow turns to gothic imagery to capture the shadowy, disorienting, uncanny quality of the *Patna* accident, comparing the "floating derelict" in question with fantastic bodies neither alive nor dead, such as a "maritime ghoul"; "wandering corpses"; and "a vampire." He claims that a collision with an abandoned wreck is so unlikely in the Arabian sea that one would almost have to attribute the accident to some evil, supernatural power – a sailor's superstition that Marlow himself quells with his comment on the collision's "aimless[ness]." The event may frustrate the human need for an explanation to the point that we might be tempted to impose some malevolent intentions where there were none. On the other hand, in the absence of certain proof, an *experienced* sailor might surmise the "exact cause" of the accident – only to uncover in that "exact cause" a paradoxical reminder of the arbitrary, meaningless nature of pure accident itself, to which anyone may be subject.

We encounter the fogginess and uncertainty of reality in Marlow's description of his unsettling, first private conversation with Jim over dinner at the Malabar Hotel after court. Jim's account of the *Patna* crisis is so anguished and so "subtle," Marlow says, that "the mystery of his attitude got hold of me as though he had been an individual in the forefront of his kind, as if the obscure truth involved were momentous enough to affect mankind's conception of itself…."[102] Potentially echoing Lingard's misjudgment of his protégé in *An Outcast*, Marlow finds Jim's "attitude" mysterious because it is strikingly antithetical to the youth who was "outwardly so typical of that good stupid kind we like to feel marching right and left of us in life."[103] However, unlike *An Outcast*'s Lingard who pushes his compassion too far when it comes to Willems, Marlow is capable of reflective distance, as his sceptical, qualifying phrases "as though" and "as if" show. He observes that Jim's promise of depth – or "mystery" – contradicts what the young man's bearing and physical characteristics would normally indicate about his character.[104] Equally, though, it could be that what appears to be profound in Jim's character is mundane. Thus Jim's surprising moral struggle shows up stable meanings – such as the usual or conventional signs of the uncomplicated, trustworthy type that he appears to be – as imposed or inscribed rather than essential and reliable.

At a seminal point in Marlow's conversation with his protégé, Jim's thinking threatens to dissolve the distinction between right and wrong that is the ground of judgment:

> "I was so lost, you know. It was the sort of thing one does not expect to happen to one. It was not like a fight, for instance."
>
> "It was not," I admitted. He appeared changed, as if he had suddenly matured.
>
> "One couldn't be sure," he muttered.
>
> "Ah! You were not sure," I said, and was placated by the sound of a faint sigh that passed between us like the flight of a bird in the night.
>
> "Well, I wasn't," he said courageously. "It was something like that wretched story they made up. It was not a lie – but it wasn't truth all the same. It was something…. One knows a downright lie. There was not the thickness of a sheet of paper between the right and the wrong of this affair."
>
> "How much more did you want?" I asked; but I think I spoke so low that he did not catch what I said. He had advanced his argument as though life had been a network of paths separated by chasms. His voice sounded reasonable.[105]

Jim recognizes in a moment of profound, maturing clarity that the crisis was inherently indeterminate – that "it was not like a fight," rendering any clear-cut decision about his course of conduct deeply uncertain if not impossible. Jim is correct – although Marlow suggests that, even though Jim was indeed harshly judged by the assessors for abandoning the ship in an impossible situation, extremely uncertain conditions do not mean that everything is permitted. Marlow knows that indeterminacy conditions the modern world – and that the problem of ethical response persists through this.[106] His realism consists of never expecting or demanding more certainty as a basis for one's conduct: action doesn't depend on total certainty, just sufficient certainty.

Ironically, Jim's desperate need for reassurance, for moral certitude, brings about an acute state of uncertainty in Marlow: Jim "wanted an ally, a helper, an accomplice. I felt the risk I ran of being circumvented, blinded, decoyed, bullied, perhaps, into taking a definite part in a dispute impossible of decision if one had to be fair to all the phantoms in possession – to the reputable that had its claims and to the disreputable that had its exigencies."[107] Jim insists that he did everything he could during the *Patna* crisis under the circumstances; but he inadvertently brings Marlow to see the validity of both the "reputable" claims on Jim's loyalty (he should have remained with his ship) on the one hand, and the "disreputable" elements of his situation (he was compelled to jump by extreme circumstances and the instinct of self-preservation) on the other. This equality coupled with Marlow's word "phantom" show there was no *real* or substantial choice between right and wrong conduct aboard the steamer; and neither "phantom" can negate or outweigh the other, constituting an opposition comparable, Marlow remarks, to that of light and darkness: "It seemed to me I was being made to comprehend the Inconceivable – and I know of nothing to compare with the discomfort of such a sensation. I was being made to look at the convention that lurks in all truth and on the essential sincerity of falsehood."[108] In Jim's situation, the conventional opposition between appearance and reality seems to be an illusion – and this is a deeply uncomfortable perspective because it suggests that there is no stable reality, no reliable truth.

Redirecting his thinking to set aside abstractions, however, Marlow attends to observable, pressing concerns and questions about the way he and others live. This turn away from abstract formulations towards experience reflects what Conrad professes, as we saw in chapter 1, to be his own particular focus: instead of "endless analysis" Conrad wants to convey characters who "bleed to prick and are moving in a visible world."[109] The shift is typical of Marlow who sees ideas as "tramps, vagabonds knocking at the back-door of your mind, each taking a little of your substance, each carrying away some crumb of that belief in a few simple notions you must cling to if you want to live decently and would like to die easy!"[110] Marlow does not explicitly state what those "few simple notions" might be – but what he calls his "confounded democratic quality of vision" comes close to demonstrating how one might morally survive the limitlessness and indeterminacy that those vagabond-like ideas represent. He dwells on the details of experience to which he applies his highly developed faculties of observation, perception, reason, and compassion. We see this in his explanation for his special involvement in Jim's – not just anyone's – life: "My weakness consists in not having a discriminating eye for the incidental – for the externals – no eye for the hod of the rag-picker or the fine linen of the next man."[111] Marlow does not deny that he discriminates between the men he meets; it's just that he doesn't judge them by "externals." His later remark about Jim's unfortunately "fine feelings" gives us insight into how one might define the "internals" for which, by his own account, Marlow possesses a "discriminating eye": "A little coarser nature would not have borne the strain; it would have had to come to terms with itself – with a sigh, with a grunt or even with a guffaw; a still coarser one would have remained invulnerably ignorant and completely uninteresting."[112] In this observation that for his own sake, Jim could do with more grit, we can see that Marlow orients his judgment not according to what he calls "incidentals" – especially conventional signs of class distinctions – but rather by what he recognizes as a person's "nature," disposition, or character. He distinguishes between the people he meets according to what he can see of their characters, that is, according to their capacity to "come to terms with itself" – "itself" referring to human nature and nature, reality in all its apparent fogginess and uncertainty.

Marlow's moderate outlook is especially apparent when we consider his perspective on Jim with Aristotle's doctrine of the mean. Again, Marlow wonders if Jim may be too "fine," while noting that a character at the other extreme would be dull and "completely uninteresting." Someone whose character falls between those opposing dispositions, such as a person with that slightly "coarser nature," would hit the mark in this situation. However, Marlow's claim is ambiguous enough to set this formulation off balance, or better yet, to resist a merely formulaic deployment of an Aristotelian outlook – a resistance that appears more explicitly or intentionally in the final Marlow novel, *Chance*, to which we will turn in chapter 5. In *Lord Jim*, Marlow's language invites his listeners to at least consider that Jim's sensitive disposition may be what enables him to endure rather than merely eclipse "the strain" or tension between realistic human imperfection and idealistic heroism. He implies that Captain Montague Brierly, an assessor at the inquiry who commits suicide shortly afterwards, is a contrasting example – a character who is unable to bear that strain or tension between imperfection and ideals. Brierly lives by the illusion that conventions – such as the naval code of honour that, he thinks, Jim reveals to be a sham – completely and reliably reflect or uphold an objective perfection in nature and human nature. Marlow recalls the captain and his flawless reputation as "present[ing] to [him] and to the world a surface as hard as granite,"[113] the result of an untarnished career that escaped the kind of accident or crisis that Jim endures. Brierly's hard intolerance contrasts with Marlow's grounded outlook on nature and human nature, whereby codes of honour cannot solve or accommodate every situation. Brierly's desperate plea to Marlow that Jim be encouraged, even paid, to abandon the court proceedings, gives us an example of real denial in contrast with *An Outcast*'s Lingard's final, judicious response to Willems's egregious betrayal and pathetic dishonesty. If Marlow leaves open the possibility that there is something admirable in Jim's apparently excessive sensitivity – for it may be the trait that forces him to encounter and suffer without falsely collapsing the tension between the ideal and the real – the very element that seems to dismantle the potential symmetry of the doctrine of the mean is itself Aristotelian.

Embedded in the first layer of Marlow's assessment of Jim – as one who would have suffered less if only he were able to accept his failings – is the idea that Jim suffers needlessly, that his moral pain stems from an illusion of honour. Jim's shame appears quaint and misguided; perhaps he needs, as Marlow's friend Chester claims, "to see things exactly as they are."[114] And yet, Marlow's echo of Chester's words is ironic, and Marlow rejects Chester's offer to help Jim – an action that rescues Jim by putting him at a distance from Chester's excessively "real" (because degraded and extremely cynical) outlook on the world and on human possibilities. The next layer of Marlow's implicitly Aristotelian formulation – again, the assertion that "a coarser nature would not have borne the strain" – keeps in view the possibility that Jim's fine sensibilities may be a strength, or that they are at least potentially worthy of high regard. There is indeed a real or true "strain" between "things as they are" and things that could be otherwise. Honour may not in itself be an illusion; rather, it may be substantial enough to create the tension that Jim is bound to suffer.[115] In short, Marlow resists the brutish cynicism where extreme scepticism can lead.

Marlow challenges a variety of frameworks typically used for appraising human conduct – as if to expose their dullness to the vibrancy of chance in human nature. Even unofficial inquiries "into the state of a man's soul" may rely on their own, implicit, and blinding ordinances. For example, Marlow anticipates his listeners' prejudices:

> I affirm he had achieved greatness; but the thing would be dwarfed in the telling, or rather in the hearing. Frankly, it is not my words that I mistrust but your minds. I could be eloquent were I not afraid you fellows had starved your imaginations to feed your bodies. I do not mean to be offensive; it is respectable to have no illusions – and safe – and profitable – and dull. Yet you too in your time must have known the intensity of life, that light of glamour created in the shock of trifles, as amazing as the glow of sparks struck from a cold stone – and as short-lived, alas![116]

Marlow wants his audience to sympathize with Jim, partly because the younger sailor appears to hold himself to a morally exacting standard when "there are men here and there to whom the whole of life is like an after-dinner hour with a cigar; easy, pleasant, empty,"[117] recalling the men Jim met in the Eastern port who, in the frame narrator's words, exercise a negative "determination to lounge safely through existence."[118] Marlow's slightly contemptuous view of his audience recalls a moment in *Heart of Darkness* when one of his listeners apparently comments that Marlow's despair at the prospect of missing his opportunity to hear Kurtz speak, was "absurd": "Here you all are, each moored with two good addresses, like a hulk with two anchors, a butcher round one corner, a policeman round another, excellent appetites, and temperature normal – you hear – normal from year's end to year's end. And you say, Absurd! Absurd be – exploded!"[119] In both instances Marlow implies that basic physical needs of security and sustenance, once fulfilled, can dull the imagination – and that the capacity to imagine one's way into another's situation or context is essential to making fair and true appraisals of conduct. He points out the safety and predictability of ongoing health and the uninterrupted comforts of middle-class, English life – reminding his audience that these are in themselves conventions that can make us forget our mortality, our own weaknesses or vulnerabilities.

Marlow points out that the conventions of religion can have the same effect as material security and convenience. We see this in Marlow's description of Jim's pastor-father and sisters in Essex, Christian "men and women peopling that quiet corner of the world as free of danger or strife as a tomb and breathing equably the air of undisturbed rectitude [...]

Nothing ever came to them; they would never be taken unawares and never be called upon to grapple with fate."[120] Marlow mocks Jim's family for their uncomplicated, unencumbered way of being in the world; their view is limited by their "clear unconscious eyes." Instead, Marlow advocates a moral vision that is paradoxically *unclear* because much more complex, an orientation towards ideals of good and right conduct coupled with an openness to the imperfections or flaws – elements of chance, risk, and accident in nature and human nature that complicate and humanize those ideals.

Another significant target is modern science where we find beneath an apparent focus on value-neutral facts a rigidly codified view – much like what Marlow witnesses in the inquiry at Jim's trial, especially in assessor Captain Brierly. We see Marlow's critique of a modern scientific framework in his lyrical description of Stein's trading post:

> there's many a heavenly body in the lot crowding upon us of a night that mankind had never heard of, it being outside the sphere of its activities and of no earthly importance to anybody but to the astronomers who are paid to talk learnedly about its composition, weight, path – the irregularities of its conduct, the aberrations of its light – a sort of scientific scandalmongering. Thus with Patusan. It was referred to knowingly in the inner government circles in Batavia, especially as to its irregularities and aberrations, and it was well known by name to some few, very few, in the mercantile world. Nobody, however, had been there, and I suspect nobody desired to go there in person, just as an astronomer, I should fancy, would strongly object to being transported into a distant heavenly body, where, parted from his earthly emoluments, he would be bewildered by the view of an unfamiliar heavens. However, neither heavenly bodies nor astronomers have anything to do with Patusan. It was Jim who went there. I only meant you to understand that had Stein arranged to send him into a star of the fifth magnitude the change could not have been greater. He left his earthly failings behind him and that sort of reputation he had, and there was a totally new set of conditions for his imaginative faculty to work upon.[121]

Astronomers find irregularities and aberrations "scandalous" or morally reprehensible; they want everything to conform perfectly to their abstract knowledge, much like the "inner government" officials assessors in Batavia (Jakarta, Indonesia) who have specialized knowledge of the area that focuses on Patusan's "irregularities and aberrations" – aspects that don't conform to their modern, professional mercantile economy. This recalls the courtroom inquiry, where the assessors – especially Brierly – treat Jim as something of an "aberration" or anomaly, an unusual type to be avoided. Marlow, on the other hand, knows that the unforeseen is always there for all of us, like the submerged wreck that collides with the *Patna*, ready to disrupt the orderly world of human affairs. He accepts our subjection to the unforeseen, without regarding human beings as passive victims radically subject to chance and accident, or as all-powerful agents who should attempt to control chance through science or rule-governed behaviour and "systems" that minimize or eliminate it. Rather, he suggests that his hypothetical astronomers and government officials lose out in their restricted outlooks: in their avoidance of so-called abnormality, they miss seeing something higher – "a view of an unfamiliar heavens."

Marlow admits to being torn between what he remembers of Jim during the *Patna* inquiry and what he witnesses in Patusan. He describes his "last view of" Jim on the island,

> – in a strong light, dominating and yet in complete accord with his surroundings – with the life of the forests and with the life of men. I own that I was impressed, but I must admit to myself that after all this is not the lasting impression. He was protected by his isolation, alone of his own superior kind, in close touch with Nature, that keeps faith on such easy terms with her lovers. But I cannot fix before my eye the image of his safety. I shall always remember him as seen through the open door of my room, taking perhaps too much to heart the mere consequences of his failure.[122]

Juxtaposing two "impression[s]" of Jim, Marlow sees a potentially unbridgeable gulf between the modern, contemporary world and the ancient sphere of action where Jim actualizes his virtues on ancient terms. There is a powerful beauty in that image of Jim's harmony with nature – a combination of nature and convention, or conventions in harmony with nature. In Patusan, Marlow can see Jim's virtues – his "superior kind" or type of character. But that wonderful image of happiness and heroism is still not powerful enough to displace Marlow's memory of Jim's anguish at his initial failure (as Jim saw it) and subsequent failure to sustain his ideals once fulfilled in Patusan. Marlow's word "failure" is weighed down by Jim's suffering and by Marlow's own failure, in a sense, to fully affirm the virtues on classical terms. His sceptical yet mournful account suggests that Jim found in Patusan an ancient, thus potentially untenable sphere of action that threatens to render Jim's successes irrelevant to our psychological and physical survival in the world as it is.

Still, Marlow offers us a way of seeing that exceeds mourning and failure. There are underlying connections between Marlow's contrasting memories of Jim as the virtuous hero in Patusan and as the youth tortured by shame in the immediate aftermath of the *Patna* inquiry. As his subsequent letter to his "privileged reader" eventually shows, Marlow's "lasting impression" ironically anticipates Jim's tragic fall. Again, his own harshest judge, Jim is paradoxically susceptible to Gentleman Brown's manipulations because of his rigid ideal of heroic action; as Marlow explains, perhaps Jim took "too much to heart the mere consequences of his failure." In other words, Jim would have suffered less if he could have accepted the fundamental realities of the human species – that we are, again as Aristotle would have it, neither gods nor beasts. Indeed, what is so admirable about Marlow is his response to the knowledge that any "fixed image" of anything, needless to say a fixed image of anyone's "safety," is too distant from the nature of things to be anything but a childish or potentially dangerous illusion. However, the novel also suggests that those agents such as Jim (and *An Outcast*'s Lingard) who are so immersed in the action – directly involved, so to speak, in political life – do not, and perhaps cannot, know and see what the spectator-artist knows and sees. To some extent, Conrad solves this conundrum by implying that Marlow's insights come from his own immersion in the mess of human affairs; he is neither a philosopher nor agent but rather grounds the philosopher's reflectiveness and insight in experience, in action.

Lord Jim: A Tale makes us see our subjection to the natural limits of mortality, time, and the sweeping force of historical change, but without nihilistic apathy on the one hand, nor the hubristic will to eliminate incertitude – chance, risk, and accident – on the other. In the next chapter, we will consider how this compellingly moderate view resurfaces as a guide to our appraisal of character and conduct in one of Conrad's under-recognized novellas – a strange tragicomedy entitled *Falk: A Reminiscence*. As I hope to show, the novella foregrounds the universal potential of the narrator's voice and outlook by leaving the narrator unnamed, while giving us an Aristotelian lens on action – between the moralist's rigid reliance on external conventions on the one hand and extreme individualism on the other.

4

The Discerning Narrator in
Falk: A Reminiscence

The logic of our conduct is always at the mercy of obscure and unforeseen impulses.[1]

I ought to have seen at once – but I did not; so difficult it is for our minds, remembering so much, informed of so much, to get in touch with the real actuality at our elbow.[2]

Conrad's novella *Falk: A Reminiscence* (1903) is normally considered a minor work – and yet it distils in a comedic key what we have seen in *An Outcast of the Islands* and *Lord Jim: A Tale* – a strikingly moderate voice and outlook that implicitly critiques modern extremes. The central narrator – an unnamed merchant seaman – shares in Marlow's compassionate, yet rational or sceptical disposition as he looks back on an episode from his youth when, as a new captain, he must lay the course between conventional, domestic security on the one hand, and unmitigated instinct or impulse, on the other. Joel R. Kehler rightly points out that critics have made too little of the tension in the novella between comedy and the absurd – the former being associated with a happy resolution typically ending in marriage as is the case here, and the latter with an "awful emptiness" lurking beneath conventions.[3] However if, as Tony Tanner eloquently claims, the captain-narrator is "trying to be in the world as it is, neither refusing it nor having had to step out of it," this effort or aspiration makes him "truly mundane" only in the non-pejorative sense.[4] As Aristotle's concept of discernment (*sŭggnomē*) will help us recognize, the novella invites admiration for the young captain-narrator's navigation between extremes.

At the outset of *Falk* we encounter two opposing yet interdependent outlooks on reality: a quasi-Nietzschean contempt for modern life as an unfulfilling, even nauseating affair, and – at the other extreme – a quasi-Rousseauvian image of the modern-romantic noble savage.[5] The novella opens with a frame narrator's melancholic reflections. He and his sailor-companions agree that even though "the sea [itself] never changes [...] the times were changed."[6] The setting suggests the change is marked by a deterioration of sorts.[7] Anticipating an "execrable" dinner at a "river hostelry" outside London, brought to them by "a decrepit old waiter [who] tottered pathetically to and fro," the frame narrator wistfully imagines "primeval man" who, "evolving the first rudiments of cookery from his dim consciousness, scorched lumps of flesh at a fire of sticks in the company of other good fellows; then, gorged and happy, sat back among the gnawed bones to tell his artless tales of experience."[8] Contrasting with this almost mythical image of a more vital existence from the distant past is the unappetizing food of the present day, served on "chipped plates" in a dining room where the floor and the sideboard are rotting away.

As if to intervene in these musings, however, a sea captain (the central, unnamed narrator), begins to speak. He has spotted a small vessel on the river Thames which prompts him to tell the others a story about his first command in the Dutch East Indies at a port in Bangkok (Krung Thep Maha Nakhon), when he found himself mediating between figures who embody the oppositions that constitute the frame narrator's introductory reflections. The captain-narrator explains that his first command was a great burden from which he had longed to escape. As a young captain, he finds a bit of solace in his friendship with a supremely conventional German captain of the ironically named *Diana*, a "world-proof" vessel for himself, his wife, four children, and niece. Hermann, with his "air of civic virtue," resembles Nietzsche's "last man": he is stolidly committed to a living a safe, comfortable, domestic existence.[9] Contrasting with Hermann is Falk – a domineering, seemingly misanthropic and impulsive man who is, as the only tugboat captain in the port, the person on whom every captain depends for safe passage out to sea. Like the young captain, Falk is a regular visitor on the *Diana*; but Falk visits for a different reason: he longs to court Hermann's niece. A crisis erupts when the captain-narrator loses his chance to get out to sea because he unintentionally alienates Falk who mistakenly believes (thanks to Hermann's intimations and local gossip) that the young captain is Falk's romantic rival. Falk ends up violently towing the *Diana* out to sea, passing over the captain-narrator who is first in line. Faced with a crisis, however, the captain-narrator seizes on a chance encounter with Falk at a local hotel to clarify things and establish himself as a mediator between the reticent tugboat captain and Hermann. The situation that requires mediation is this: Falk feels that before proposing he must confess that, ten years earlier, he endured an accident at sea and resorted to cannibalism to preserve his life. And so, Falk ironically comes to depend on the young captain – given the latter's friendship with Hermann – to persuade Hermann to approve of Falk's proposal.[10] The captain-narrator listens to Falk's private testimony, and prudently facilitates a happy union by appealing to what he observes of Hermann's self-interested pragmatism, all the while having forged an alliance with the tugboat captain thus securing his own ship's departure.

The sea is, as the captain-narrator explains, "tragic and comic" – rich with chance, risk, and accident. Indeed, he suggests that the unforeseeable will at some point naturally or inevitably challenge any orderly, safe existence: "I have known the sea too long to believe in its respect for decency. An elemental force is ruthlessly frank."[11] In this case, Falk's confession – rather than a storm at sea – is the "elemental force" that disrupts Hermann's "world-proof" life. The "ruthless disclosure" tests Hermann's limitations: theft exists within his moral compass; cannibalism at sea does not – at least, he is determined to maintain a barrier against the "secrets of the sea," an ironic reflection of his lack of conviction in the strength of the rigid conventions by which he lives.[12] But, as Aristotle helps us see, it isn't simply that there is a better, third way between Hermann's excessive conventionality and Falk's apparently primal self-sufficiency. Rather, the captain narrator learns how to find the moderate, *realistic* middle ground through a shift in perspective on each figure – a compassionate yet rational humanization of each extreme.

Recasting "The Last Man"

The young captain may find the *Diana* a comforting escape from the numerous problems he faces when he takes up a post aboard a ship whose previous captain "had died suddenly;[13] but he is also critical of Hermann's "world-proof" existence,[14] leading us to see what Tony Tanner describes as "the man who clings to the shore, whose life is public and orthodox and unhaunted, who stays within the prescribed tastes of the community."[15] The captain's first command begins without any stores, an aloof first mate, and a second mate who "was, without exception, the stupidest man I had ever seen on board ship," and a "sickly [choleric] crew."[16] The situation worsens when, in desperation, he hires a man who turns out to be a thief whom Hermann tries and fails to chase down. For relief from such difficulties – and from his own self-berating thoughts – the captain relies on evening visits aboard Hermann's "innocent old ship" from which "the sea and all nautical affairs seemed very far removed."[17] Still, he shows ambivalence about his refuge when he compares the ship to a farmhouse[18] and likens Hermann to "a well-to-do farmer" and a "small shop-keeper."[19] The *Diana* recalls "the wooden plough of our forefathers" while her stern resembles "the tail end of a miller's wagon," and her curtained stern ports look like country cottage windows.[21] Reinforcing a domestic atmosphere that is closer to what the narrator calls a "pampered" life on land than life at sea is Hermann's preoccupation with family, money, and comforts of smoking, beer, and "good stout flannel" – all details that ironize the ship's name.

The captain-narrator's sardonic remark that the *Diana* is "of Bremen, not Ephesus"[20] signals a humorous disdain for Hermann and his domestic comforts that recalls Nietzsche's description of "the last man" – a contemptible figure who has given up desire and heroic suffering in favour of comfort and warmth.[22] The last man lives a long because safe, thus mediocre, existence that speaks to what Daphna Erdinast-Vulcan describes as Hermann's ironic "virtues of bourgeois capitalism."[23] The captain-narrator describes the Hermann family's laundry:

> The afternoon breeze would incite to a weird and flabby activity all that crowded mass of clothing, with its vague suggestions of drowned, mutilated and flattened humanity. Trunks without heads waved at you, arms without hands; legs without feet kicked fantastically with collapsible flourishes; and there were long white garments, that taking the wind fairly through their neck openings edged with lace, became for a moment violently distended as by the passage of obese and invisible bodies.[24]

Implied here is a form of cannibalism more horrific than the cannibalism *in extremis* to which Falk later confesses. The ghostly garments animated by the wind connote not simply death but something potentially worse – a "flattened humanity" that indicates a cannibalization of human spiritedness. The narrator sees beheaded and dismembered bodies – bodies without the capacity to think or act; he describes a "grotesque riot," an absurd chaos of bodies that are both "invisible," suggesting absence, and "obese," suggesting excessive presence. The problem is that the *Diana* is "high-walled and as solid as an institution, on the smooth level of the water, the most uninspiring and respectable craft upon the seas, useful and ugly, devoted to the support of domestic virtues like any grocer's shop on shore."[25] The captain-narrator associates the ship with a paradoxically active avoidance of life – with Hermann's dedication to the (illusory) permanence, order, and respectability of an "institution," in this case that of the family. The ship sails only on "the smooth level of the water" without having to experience or confront the challenges of nature's variability.

Hermann's initial response to Falk's confession that he has "eaten man" is typical of Nietzsche's last man who is willing to subvert the truth to maintain the comfortable condition of agreeability. Hermann is mostly upset not by the truth itself but by Falk's decision to share his story in the first place: "'Why tell?' he cried. 'Who was asking him?' It showed Falk's brutality because after all he had selfishly caused him (Hermann) much pain. He would have preferred not to know that such an unclean creature had been in the habit of caressing his children. He hoped I would say nothing of all this ashore, though. He wouldn't like it to get about that he had been intimate with an eater of men – a common cannibal."[26] Thus Hermann comically manages to see even cannibalism through the lens of his concern for his social reputation. Locating "cannibalism" in colonialist discourse, Harry Sewlall shows how Hermann uses the term in order to sustain his "bourgeois value system."[27] Nietzsche targets this kind of disavowal, declaring that "the 'general welfare' is not the sphere of truth; for truth demands to be declared even if it is ugly and unethical."[28] Falk's offence to "the general welfare" is twofold: he chooses his own life at the cost of another man's, and imposes the difficult truth about his act of self-preservation upon others. Raising the question, "is Hermann's horror at the act of cannibalism itself, or at Falk's decision to tell them about it?,"[29] Paul Vlitos points out that Hermann's real horror is fuelled by a refusal to relinquish his settled worldview.

The novella suggests, however, that all this contempt – a dehumanizing extreme – can be tempered by recognition and self-recognition. Whereas the captain-narrator may – as Tony Tanner observes – present Hermann as an embodiment of "utilitarianism, defensive abuse, and the preference for concealment," this harsh, almost vituperative perspective changes in a process that accounts for the combination of seriousness and levity in the narrator's mature, retrospective voice.[30] Even at the time, he is conscious of his own desire to abandon the pressing difficulties of his real-world problems, remarking that "I was glad to make my escape on board that Bremen *Diana*."[31] He also admires Hermann's readiness to chase down the thief – the event that begins their friendship. His story shows that when the opportunity for action arises, Herman demonstrates an impulsive generosity, a desire to help at least in a crisis (theft) with which he could sympathize. It is in dialogue or conversation, however, where the captain-narrator comes to a humanizing insight into Hermann's reaction to Falk:

"What is it you said I was last night? You know:" – he asked after some preliminary talk. "Too – too – I don't know. A very funny word."

"Squeamish?" I suggested.

"Yes. What does it mean?"

"That you exaggerate things – to yourself. Without inquiry, and so on."[32]

An English colloquialism, "squeamish," captures Hermann's limitations and prompts him to know or see them.[33] Hermann's visceral reaction is petty; he lacks the courage required to hear the difficult details of another's experience when those details challenge his views or threaten the conventions he lives by – but this may all come down to the simple, common human prudishness. The captain-narrator suggests a remedy: Hermann need only learn to practice "inquiry" – to ask questions of Falk; to balance emotional defensiveness with reason; and to allow his sense of the world to be changed by encounters with difference.

Falk's Alternative

If Hermann's retreat from the world comes across as a futile effort to eradicate risk and chance from his life, Falk's apparent self-sufficiency is an initially appealing alternative. Much of Falk's appeal is his seeming aloofness to economic concerns and social pressures at the seaport. Unlike the narrator who is burdened with worry and self-doubt, Falk seems above it all. For example, the gossipy hotelier Schomberg practices an intense resentment for the tugboat captain who (exasperatingly) won't order meat like the other "white men," but Falk doesn't appear to care about offending anyone: "It was very funny to see Schomberg ignoring him pointedly. The artificiality of it contrasted strongly with Falk's natural unconcern."[34] It is as if Falk exposes the phoniness of social conventions – making us see that they are grounded not in genuine mutual concern but in self-interest: "The truth is that being a monopolist he was under no necessity to be amiable. He was sure to get his own extortionate terms out of me for towage whether he frowned or smiled."[35] In contrast with Hermann's hypocritical perspective where, as we have seen, he prefers the *status quo*, Falk embodies a "natural," literal and direct sense of honesty: "There was no duplicity in that man."[36] And when the captain-narrator suggests it would be unnecessary to tell Hermann about the accident, he explains that "I fancied I had said something immoral. [Falk] shook his head negatively. It had to be told."[37] Falk's impulse to speak the truth contrasts with Hermann's self-serving interest in erecting a barrier against it.

In opposition to Hermann's "last-man" like conventionality, Falk demonstrates a freedom from convention that the novella implicitly critiques while acknowledging its appeal. The narrator helplessly wonders at Falk's "conduct in matters of business, which seemed to me totally unrestrained by morality or even by the commonest sort of decency."[38] At the outset, however, the narrative suggests that the young captain's awe before this state of instinctive amorality is an outlook he must overcome to assume his first command:

> he reminded me somehow of an engraving in a little book I had as a boy, which represented centaurs at a stream, and there was one, especially in the foreground, prancing bow and arrows in hand, with regular severe features and an immense curled wavy beard, flowing down his breast [...] Besides, he was a composite creature. Not a man-horse, it is true, but a man-boat [...] In the last rays of the setting sun, you could pick out far away down the reach his beard borne high up on the white structure, foaming up-stream to anchor for the night.[39]

Viewing Falk from a distance, "far away down the reach," the captain-narrator finds it easy to idealize a figure who seems to be in perfect command of his ship and his surroundings. Falk's "flowing" beard – which the narrator mentions twice – conveys a centaur-like sensuality. Comparable to a figure in a child's "little book," the image reflects the captain-narrator's youthful desire for the total, impossible freedom of effortless union with the environment that recalls what we saw in the previous chapter of Jim's illusory, pre-lapsarian state.

The central, practical problem, though, is that Falk appears to have all the control. The young captain's ship, like Hermann's, is of "a certain draught of water" that prevents both men from independently loading all their cargo due to an inconvenient sand bar at the mouth of the river. They face a potential crisis when Falk impulsively disregards the rules, refusing to tow his supposed rival's ship, and recklessly taking the *Diana* before she is prepared to leave. The young captain is ill-equipped to get himself out to sea – not least because he has only an abstract knowledge of the necessary "operations" for such a task: he doesn't know the river at all; and he doesn't yet know his ship. He explains, "I had never handled her in my life. A misunderstanding between a man and his ship, in a difficult river with no room to make it up, is bound to end in trouble for the man."[40] Moreover, many of his crew are ill, underlining the urgent need to get everyone out to sea before the entire crew catches "any tropical disease going" on shore.[41] The crisis intensifies when he attempts to gain some local knowledge of the river from the only possible source apart from Falk, only to find in a short journey into what appears to be the corrupt, subterranean world of the seaport that his only potential source of information – a man named "Johnson" – is completely unreliable and directs him to Falk for help anyway.

If the captain-narrator resists succumbing to the comforts of a Hermann-like retreat from reality, he also must extricate himself from his helpless position in order to save his ship and crew. Just as he comes to a compassionate yet sceptical understanding of Hermann, here we get a more complex, sympathetic outlook on Falk who turns out to be surprisingly conventional. The narrator learns that Falk is not above ordinary human vulnerabilities: he is concerned about his "respectability, of being like everybody else," while being "panicked" at the thought of Schomberg's lies, protesting that "this fellow is always making out something wrong, and can never rest till he gets somebody to believe him."[42] Most significantly, he discovers that the apparently autonomous, self-sufficient Falk has "found it more and more difficult to live alone."[43] Suggested here is the famous claim in the *Politics* that human beings are social, by nature: "man is a political animal."[44] Falk's outward individualism does not preclude a natural need of companionship. His quasi-Rousseauvian instinct for "self-preservation" includes a longing for intimacy with another person; he is "political" insofar as he is predisposed by nature to live in relation to others. Indeed, this predisposition, powerfully awakened in Falk by Hermann's compassionate niece, is antecedent to the basic will to live. Falk's isolation and loneliness drive him to "'wish'" that he had died at sea, that "'the crowbar [of his rival] had smashed [his] skull ten years ago.'"[45] The captain-narrator explains that Falk "had always desired a home [...] He was domestic; there had been difficulties; but since he had seen Hermann's niece he found that it had become at last impossible to live by himself. 'I mean – impossible,' [...] the world fell into my mind with the force of a new idea."[46] The new idea is, ironically enough, a very old one: "self-preservation" includes interdependency. We find it in Aristotle's *Nicomachean Ethics* where he conceives of friendship (*philia*) as any bond within and beyond family,[47] and in Aristotle's use of "political" to refer to the human need of others, for happiness or flourishing.[48] Falk's word "impossible" resonates with the narrator so deeply because it underlines an idea to which Marlow, in Conrad's *Chance*, will later articulate with characteristic irony: the unavoidably social nature of the human species.[49]

The young captain's success is contingent on his ability to humanize Falk – by dispelling myth with closeness. He seizes on a chance to help Falk escape Schomberg's "irrepressible loquacity" by guiding Falk to the hotel verandah, just as he realizes that Falk will not speak unless their conversation is private. The captain-narrator – proud of his own "presence of mind" – finds a way to evade the nosey patrons who are "crowding the windows," by appealing to what he has observed about the hotelier's self-interest: "'Hallo,' I said instantly in a loud and naïve tone, 'somebody's breaking your windows, Schomberg. Would you please tell one of your boys to bring out here a pack of cards and a couple of lights? And two long drinks, will you?'"[50] The card game shields their conversation – for the patrons, billiard players themselves, assume that the two men are only gambling. Recalling Marlow's controversial, compassionate lie to Kurtz's Intended in *Heart of Darkness*, the narrator lies to Falk under the guise of sharing a "confidence" with him about being engaged to another girl.[51] The captain-narrator then accepts Falk's request that he become a mediator between Hermann and Falk – a situation that solidifies his alliance with the man he desperately needs to save his first command. Thus the card game does not symbolize the narrator's corruption – his participation in "the game of lying, cheating, and double-dealing that makes up the daily life in an eastern port";[52] instead, it reflects a realistic outlook on ethical action that contrasts with Falk's literal, naïve belief the truth as something that must be shared and spoken always, at all costs. At the novella's end, the narrator humorously remarks on the irony of the card game and the stories that circulate about it: everyone believes that Falk arbitrarily "won" Hermann's niece from the captain, purely out of luck, whereas the game was in itself irrelevant, a performance that preserves Falk's reputation at the port.

As Daphna Erdinast-Vulcan claims, *Falk*'s "narrator should be evaluated against his apparently stronger rival." Perhaps, however, the story leads us to see that his superiority to Falk arises not only from his participation in a "community of discourse," but also with his developing, moderate – thus higher – knowledge of human nature. The young captain learns to combine reason and instinct by following his impulses judiciously, unlike Falk who is so easily carried along by emotions. Even this outlook on prudence and judiciousness is itself moderate as we see the captain-narrator come close to losing Falk's trust, when he accuses the tugboat captain of past misconduct before hearing all the facts. Recognizing his error – commenting that "the logic of our conduct is always at the mercy of obscure and unforeseen impulses"[53] – the captain-narrator implies we may not be able to rationally account for everything that we do. On the other hand, this does not mean – as Hermann believes – that accident or the unforeseen inherently threaten happiness.

The Discerning Narrator

Aristotle can help us recognize that the captain-narrator's attempt to comprehend Falk's suffering abandons the rigid moralizing we witness in Hermann without abandoning judgment altogether. The narrator practices what Aristotle calls discernment – a way of seeing defined by equitable, fair, compassionate judgment or appraisal of character and conduct.[54] The captain-narrator demonstrates this form of appraisal when he and imagines his way into Falk's world instead of imposing a strict moral code or commonplace opinions (*doxa*) onto Falk, and by pursuing the truth about what has occurred.[55] Much like Marlow in *Lord Jim,* the young captain wants to get to the truth of the matter – so that this truth might be shared to contest Hermann's emotional, opinionated response that the novella guides us to see as understandable but unfair. As he explains, "I fancy it [asking Falk questions and listening to the narrative that emerges from them] was the only way I could that night have stood by him."[56] Aristotle can shed light on the captain-narrator's pursuit of contextual understanding: in the *Nicomachean Ethics*, as Martha Nussbaum explains, Aristotle defines discernment [*suggnōmē*] as "a gentle art of particular perception, a temper of mind that refuses to demand retribution without knowing the whole story."[57] Nussbaum adds that "in [Aristotle's] *Rhetoric* [...] *suggnōmē*, 'judging with,' [...] typically suggests the idea of forgiveness, in a way that connects etymologically with the idea of the sharing of the other person's point of view."[58] "Judging with" sounds very much like the captain-narrator's intersubjective practice of "stand[ing] by" Falk; this practice – as Nussbaum's language indicates – is not precisely "forgiveness," despite the usefulness of the term in orienting our understanding of *suggnōmē*. Whereas forgiveness refers to blameworthy wrong-doing, Aristotle's term refers to a transgression that is not blameworthy because it exceeds ethics (which involves a real choice or decision).[59] This distinction applies to Falk for, as Walter E. Anderson observes, "he clearly feels no guilt and does not desire forgiveness";[60] and the story does not lead us to see this absence of "guilt" as a moral failure. Rather, Falk's absence of guilt; his obvious feelings of regret; and his blatant unconcern about local gossip show that he knows he transgressed in some fundamental, but unavoidable, way.[61] At issue is not simply the fact that Falk knowingly transgressed, but rather that his actions fall under one of

Aristotle's categories for *suggnōmē*: "overstraining of human nature."[62] Hermann's misguidedly absolute judgment of Falk is an instructive counterexample – similar to Schomberg's misguided conclusion that Falk is "miserly and envious"[63] based on Falk's vegetarianism and preference for dining alone.

Listening attentively to Falk's recollection of the events aboard the *Borgmester Dahl*, the narrator develops a sense of the whole. He intentionally clears away the associations and assumptions accumulated not from experience but from information gathered from newspaper reports[64] and books: "Remembering the things one reads of it was difficult to realise the true meaning of his answers. I ought to have *seen* at once – but I did not; so difficult it is for our minds, remembering so much, instructed so much, informed of so much, to get in touch with the real actuality at our elbow."[65] This outlook on reading marks a shift from what we saw of the captain's initial tendency to see Falk through the lens of his recollection of the engraving in a book from childhood. Now, the captain-narrator juxtaposes "true meaning" with "things one reads of" and a cluttered mind; he seeks a particular way of thinking that is "difficult" because it sheds the apparent safety of received ideas and enters an intensely unpredictable dialogue where anything might be spoken or revealed. He recalls his effort to get to "the real actuality" by moving "from question to question," seeking "the whole story."[66] This attentive disposition turns away from preconceptions and towards genuine thinking and equitable judgment – an example of what Aristotle describes in the *Poetics* as reading and appraising a poet's words in context to derive their meaning.[67] Whereas Hermann judges Falk's action in isolation, the narrator, in listening to Falk's story, "witnessed [Falk's] physical struggles, seeing the working of the rack and hearing the true voice of pain."[68] A Rousseauvian reading may tell us that Falk's cry of pain is "true" because it is primal thus uncivilized: it precedes language, which necessarily enters conventions and the information gathered from reading and memory that the narrator implies will lead to restrictive because conventional judgments.[69] And yet, the narrator uses the word "voice" (rather than "cry") – a term that suggests, when considered with Aristotle, a particularly human, rather than a merely animal or primal sound.[70] Aristotle would argue that Falk's cry is "true" because it expresses his pain at recalling and reliving an impossible dilemma: his natural instinct to survive forced him to transgress a natural human limit. [71] Positioning himself as an attentive listener who invites Falk to tell his story by moving (again), from "question to question," the narrator wants to know not merely about Falk's feelings but a way to read them truthfully.

It cannot be merely coincidental that Hermann does not tell his own stories.[72] Only when the young captain has a story to share does Hermann narrate out of necessity to translate it into German for his wife. Whereas "tales of heroism at sea" portray human character and action in extraordinary, unforeseen circumstances, the novella associates Hermann's rigid approach to chance or the unforeseen and unpredictable – his claim that "no circumstances could excuse a crime"[73] – with a non-literary disposition. Narrative requires that storyteller and listener retain, to make connections between, myriad details and nuances – whereas the captain-narrator's final observation about the Hermann family is that they are unable to think beyond the immediate present. Even after they had on the previous day witnessed their niece's happiness, Hermann comments that Mrs. Hermann doesn't know "whether a man of that sort could make a girl happy"; and so the captain-narrator remarks that "these good people did not seem to be able to retain an impression for a whole twelve hours."[74] The comment shows affectionate good humour, but it also emphasizes the novella's serious preoccupation with literary narrative's unique capacity to meditate on matters of character, conduct, and human nature.

The *Borgmester Dahl* incident occurred three decades before the captain-narrator tells the story to his present listeners; even so, he reconstructs the story with a sense of immediacy that would be impossible without having genuinely sympathized with Falk. Vividly conveying conditions of extreme duress, the narrator appeals not only to shared mortality but to the more specific idea of overstrained human nature as a ground of understanding. Not long after departure the crew found several barrels were rotten and had to be thrown overboard,[75] while human error in combination with a storm destroyed the rest: "On one frightful night, when they expected their hulk to turn over with them every moment, a heavy sea broke on board, deluged the store-rooms and spoiled the best part of the remaining provisions. It seems the hatch had not been properly secured. This instance of neglect is characteristic of utter discouragement."[76] Rather than condemn the crew for the apparent neglect of the hatch, the captain-narrator discerns in this detail an atmosphere of "utter discouragement" or despair – the crew's understandable demoralization under extreme circumstances. Equally compassionate is his insight into the dehumanizing effects of starvation. Two men steal away in their last remaining boat – originally prepared for six sailors as their final hope of finding help – and this last "extremity [...] seems easier to bear, because of the direct danger of the seas. The confined space [...] the imminent menace of the waves, seem to draw men together, in spite of madness, suffering and despair. But there was a ship [...] pervaded, ruled, and possessed by the pitiless spectre of starvation."[77] Men will easily forge an alliance against a storm, an external force of nature – but hunger, an invisible, internal foe is inevitably fractious. Starvation is what Aristotle describes as "a certain frightening thing that is too much for a human being to bear."[78] A concrete example of hunger's dehumanizing effects can be found in *Heart of Darkness*: "No fear can stand up to hunger, no patience can wear it out, disgust simply does not exist where hunger is; and as to [...] what you may call principles, they are less than chaff in the breeze."[79] *Falk* implies that this aspect of human nature – the tortuously reductive experience of overwhelming hunger – is the proper context for understanding the transgressor's conduct.

Much like Jim's conduct aboard the *Patna* before his fateful leap, Falk's conduct during the crisis distinguishes him from his fellow sailors and even his captain. When the crew discovers that many of their provisions were spoiled, "Falk tried to inspire some energy into his captain but failed."[80] We learn that when the sailors disappeared with the last boat – with the only remaining means locating another ship – Falk took charge – advising the captain to "'Shoot, sir! Shoot them down! [...] and I will jump overboard to regain the boat.' But the captain, after taking aim with an irresolute arm, turned suddenly away."[81] And when "the organized life of the ship had come to an end [...] it was Falk who took in hand the distribution of such food as remained."[82] Falk's effort to maintain order and to sustain hope recall the courageous person who "is as undaunted as a human being can be. He will fear things [...] but he will endure them in the way that he ought and as reason commands, for the sake of the noble, for this is the end of virtue."[83] If Falk's "heart revolted against the horror of death and he said to himself that he would struggle for every precious minute of his life,"[84] his actions demonstrated a sense of duty and readiness to act under extreme circumstances that complicates even the captain-narrator's claim that Falk embodies "the law [...] of self-preservation" – an instinctive desire to save himself.[85]

Falk: A Reminiscence makes us see the nature of nature – what the frame-narrator describes as "the sea that never changes," ironically noting that "its works for all the talk of men are wrapped in mystery."[86] The "mystery" is one way of describing that element of uncertainty, that which escapes our "talk," language, knowledge, and order. Hermann's response to the "mystery" is to retreat from it in an attempt eradicate the unforeseeable – a futile thus pathetic endeavour. Although appealingly closer to nature – an appeal that Hermann's niece shares despite "the worn-out earth of our possession"[87] – Falk comes to embody pathos at the other extreme. His repeated use of the word "misfortune" and its cognates, appearing at least a dozen times in the text, emphasizes the pathos of his situation. Between these extremes the captain-narrator's humanity – his knowingly humorous perspective – stems from what he learned in the episode he relates: nature can reduce us to passivity, death being the ultimate reminder of that fact; but this does not mean that all our attempts to bring order to the world are futile. Like Jim in Patusan before Gentleman Brown's arrival, the captain seizes on unpredictable events, turning them into opportunities to bring two goods into equilibrium, in this case a wedding engagement on the one hand, and the safe passage of a ship and crew on the other. Whereas *Lord Jim* draws attention to the difference between the philosophical storyteller and the life of action through Marlow and Jim respectively, *Falk* does not explore this distinction but rather emphasizes that the higher knowledge of nature and human nature that we encounter in Marlow and the Marlovian captain-narrator of the novel arises from experience – from action. Put differently, literature loves chance because it is deeply, often paradoxically, preoccupied with the nature of reality. Conrad's late-career novel, *Chance: A Tale in Two Parts* – the focus of the next chapter – contains a joyous affirmation of the literary narrator's higher knowledge of nature and human nature, what Marlow, recalling Aristotle, calls "practical sagacity."

5

Marlow's Practical Wisdom:
Chance: A Tale in Two Parts

"Listen, Powell," I said. "We got to know each other by chance?"

"Oh, quite!" he admitted, adjusting his hat.

"And the science of life consists in seizing every chance that presents itself," I pursued. "Do you believe that?"

"Gospel truth," he declared innocently.

"Well, don't forget it."[1]

"You remember," went on Marlow, "how I feared that Mr. Powell's want of experience would stand in his way of appreciating the unusual [...] I may well have doubted the capacity of a young man too much concerned with the creditable performance of his duties to observe what in the nature of things is not easily observable in itself, and still less so under the special circumstances."[2]

"I think that I have no sagacity – no practical sagacity."[3]

In *An Outcast of the Islands*, *Lord Jim*, and *Falk: A Reminiscence*, Conrad's narrators and the stories they tell remind us that we are neither all-powerful gods nor pathetic beasts, but mortal beings who are vulnerable yet capable of action. In these three works we see a searching, reflexive affirmation of this middle ground – where our subjection to chance is not opposed to, but rather part of, the genuine agency that conditions human flourishing and happiness. For Conrad's most overt expression of what we have come to recognize as a moderate outlook on nature and human nature in his fiction, let us turn to the fourth and final Marlow novel: *Chance: A Tale in Two Parts* (1913). John G. Peters defends the somewhat contested idea that there is a significant difference between Conrad's early- and late-career versions of Marlow,[4] arguing that in *Chance* "the universe [...] lacks the overall incomprehensibility of the earlier Marlow's world positing, instead, a limited incomprehensibility based upon the unpredictability of chance."[5] Ultimately, writes Peters, the novel contains the idea that "human beings cannot escape the effects of chance, and while events are unpredictable that does not imply an absurd universe."[6] In part, this apparent change in Marlow's worldview may suit his character in the most pragmatic way: he is older now, more experienced – less preoccupied with the instability or elusiveness of the truth, and more focused on chance opportunities for human happiness that we must, as he advises his friend, learn to recognize so we can "seize" upon them. Marlow is wise and excellent – but he embodies a distinctively human wisdom and excellence: humanization is built into Conrad's frame narratives, where readers can hear and see the unique qualities and contours of the situated narrator's humanity.

Chance is framed by remarks that invite us to meditate on the relationship between chance and human flourishing or happiness. In the first chapter we meet three seamen having dinner at a Thames-side inn: a semi-retired Marlow; Marlow's friend who is also the unnamed frame narrator; and their younger "new acquaintance" Charles Powell.[7] Recalling the riverside setting and atmosphere of dissatisfaction at the beginning of *Falk*, Powell contrasts "the slovenly manner in which the dinner was served" with the "efficient" work of the sea. On shore, workers have a "sense" or illusion of "security" that potentially leads to complacency and poor results.[8] A sailor's proximity to nature, on the other hand, teaches him how to live with the unforeseeable – chance, risk, or accident – as an inescapable yet sometimes fortuitous aspect of reality, and this, Powell claims, means a potentially high level of conduct. The discussion implies a critique of risk-averse outlooks on the unforeseeable and an affirmation of chance that resurfaces at the end of the novel, when Marlow urges Powell to act on his feelings and risk proposing to his beloved recently widowed friend, Flora de Barral. We meet Flora in Part I, where Marlow tells the frame-narrator about her – having been inspired to do so by Powell's story about how he acquired his first post as a second officer under the command of Roderick Anthony, the brother-in-law of Marlow's summertime friend and chess partner, Mr. John Fyne. Having been virtually orphaned by her now-imprisoned father, and abused and abandoned by her governess, Flora lives with the Fynes until she elopes with Captain Anthony. John and especially Zoë disapprove of the union, uncharitably fearing that Flora merely wants a means of providing for her father upon his release from prison. In Part II Marlow once again meets Powell Jr. who continues his story about his first post, describing the journey itself – the *Ferndale* on its way to Africa (transporting dynamite) with Captain Anthony, Flora (now Mrs. Anthony), and Flora's father, Mr. de Barral. Aboard the ship Powell witnesses de Barral's attempt to poison the captain, a charade that ends with de Barral's death when he drinks the poison instead. Six years later Anthony dies in a collision at sea, leaving Flora a widow thus free to remarry. Just as *Falk*'s narrator comedically facilitates the marriage between Falk and Hermman's niece, Marlow recognizes an opportunity for Powell and Flora's happiness, and encourages the characters to be open about their mutual affection. In the novel's closing lines, Marlow expects to hear of Powell and Flora's wedding.

Aristotle's theory of practical wisdom gives us a framework for reading *Chance* as part of Conrad's ongoing preoccupation with literature's unique means of making us see. As Aristotle explains in the *Nicomachean Ethics*, practical wisdom (*phronesis*) is not exactly a science, which is focused on unchanging truths, and not exactly an art, which involves making. Because human life is various and mutable the right course of action in a particular situation is often not obvious; we are always deliberating about what do because human living inherently "admit[s] of being otherwise."[9] Ethics is something like "the most fundamental of the sciences" – "that which discerns for what end each thing must be done. And this is the good for each thing, and in general the best in all natures."[10] Marlow captures this similarity when he refers to happiness not as a science but as "a science of *life*," which seems to come down to the capacity to see – that is, to "observe what in the nature of things is not so easily observable in itself."[11] And yet, Marlow outwardly denies that he possesses "practical sagacity," mocking the term when a friend ascribes the virtue to him. Aristotle's theory of practical wisdom will help us see that Conrad's rejection of the term amounts to a rejection not of practical wisdom but of philosophical language and knowledge, which always risks hardening into an impediment to the perceptiveness that his fiction compels us to admire. As I hope to show in what follows, Marlow rejects modern consequentialism and rule-bound ethics in favour of character and intention which are central to practical wisdom; and this outlook forms part of the novel's defence of a literary outlook on human beings as subject but irreducible to contingency and chance.

"Mediocrity Is Our Mark": Marlow's Sceptical Wisdom

Distinguishing between philosophy and practical wisdom, Aristotle deems the former unhelpful when it comes to human living, where we have agency and our subjection to chance. Our lives are "bound up with action, accompanied with reason, and concerned with things good and bad for a human being."[12] We admire the person with practical wisdom (*phronimos*) for readily discerning what to do in to a given context or "relative to us."[13] To find the mean – to hit the mark of right action – a person must feel and act "when one ought and at the things one ought, in relation to those people whom one ought, for the sake of what and as one ought."[14] The doctrine of the mean is a guide – but those who truly possess practical wisdom fully embody it; their capacity to see what is required has become part of who they are.[15] Indeed, an application of merely theoretical knowledge will likely lead to mistakes, because these would be rules which – by definition – we would indiscriminately apply to every situation.[16] Stephen Salkever explains: "What is uniquely human is that our potentialities are many and varied and by no means always compatible or consistent with one another. This lack of strict biological definition is both a strength and a problem for us" that Aristotelian ethics tries to address.[17] But literary narratives can show us character in action, including what Aristotle teaches, which is that those who desire practical wisdom need time and experience to fulfil this aspiration.[18]

As if laying the groundwork for an alternative ethics, Marlow exposes the shortcomings of commonplace views on action. At the novel's outset Marlow points out in conversation with his friend Powell Jr. the insufficiency of consequence or outcome as a measure of right action. Indeed, Marlow himself embodies what Aristotle calls "correctness of thinking" – rather than "correctness of opinion" – where the emphasis is on process rather than a desired consequence.[19] In the novel's first chapter, for example, the frame narrator recounts Marlow's conversation with Powell who reminisces about the immediate aftermath of his certification with the British Merchant Marine: by a series of chance events, his first berth was with Captain Anthony. Looking back, Powell wonders at the shipping master – also coincidentally named Powell, just as Marlow and his friend Powell share the first name Charles – who refused to accept the young seaman's gratitude for setting him up with his first post. Instead of accepting thanks, Powell Sr. had pointed to the circumstances that led to the position – arguing at the time that the young sailor may as well thank the dynamite in the *Ferndale*'s cargo that necessitated the voyage in the first place. Recalling that Powell Sr. repeatedly refused the younger Powell's thanks with the claim that "'the voyage isn't finished yet,' Powell remarks, 'Queer man. As if it made any difference. Queer man.'"[20]

Prompted by his interlocutor's bewilderment, Marlow indirectly teaches "correctness in thinking" by re-situating the discussion in terms of intention and responsibility. Daniel Brudney defines this ability as the virtue of "attentiveness to the other," noting a younger Marlow's "failure to extend that virtue far enough" in the case of the Intended in *Heart of Darkness*.[21] In *Chance*, Marlow does not leap to a conclusion but imagines his way into the situation while making his focus clear: intrinsic, character-driven intentions and motives.[22] He initially responds to Powell by advising that "it's certainly unwise to admit any sort of responsibility for our actions, whose consequences we are never able to foresee."[23] This insight echoes Conrad's own claim in his Author's Note to *Chance* where he asserts, "it is only for their intentions that men can be held responsible. The ultimate effects of whatever they do are far beyond their control."[24] But Marlow adds an ironic dimension to, or insight into, this claim. It may be "unwise" to *admit* responsibility for our actions given that we only have our intentions (that many factors come into play in the real world that affect outcomes) – but this does not mean that we are absolved of responsibility or that everything is permitted. The point is moderate rather than merely ambiguous: even though we must recognize the role of chance in the outcome of our actions, we are moral agents.

Initially Powell responds rather defensively to Marlow's sceptical view of Powell Sr.: "'The consequence of his action was that I got a ship' [...] 'That could not do much harm,' he added with a laugh which argued a probably unconscious contempt for general ideas."[25] Young Powell's argument runs like this: a young sailor has work, and a captain now has what he requires for a voyage. In this view the shipping master might indeed appear prudent – recalling the captain-narrator in *Falk* whose actions simultaneously ensure his own safe passage and happiness for Hermann's niece and Falk. However, Marlow points out the limitations of a consequentialist view of action:

> "Oh I wouldn't suggest," he said, "that your name-sake, Mr. Powell, the Shipping Master, had done you much harm [...] He was but a man, and the incapacity to achieve anything distinctly good or evil is inherent in our earthly condition. Mediocrity is our mark. And perhaps it's just as well, since, for the most part, we cannot be certain of the effect of our actions."
>
> "I don't know about the effect," the other stood up to Marlow manfully. "What effect did you expect anyhow? I tell you he did something uncommonly kind."
>
> Marlow retorted gently [...] "I cannot help thinking that there was some malice in the way he seized the opportunity to serve you [...] I am inclined to think your cheek alarmed him. And this was an excellent occasion to suppress you altogether [...] The notice was too uncommonly short. But under the circumstances you'd have covered yourself with ignominy."[26]

Marlow's analysis gives us a context for understanding his later advice to Powell, that happiness or "the science of life" hinges on our ability to "seize" opportunities for action. He sheds a sceptical light not on Powell Sr.'s seizing an opportunity to help the younger Powell, but on "the way" he did so. Marlow's focus on intention distinguishes him from what, if taken out of context, may appear to advocate indiscriminate or arbitrary action, a kind of groundless, quasi-Nietzschean affirmation of life itself. Instead, Marlow tempers his friend's focus on outcome or effect, by echoing Powell's use of the word "harm" and gently introducing the qualifier "much" to suggest Powell Sr.'s seemingly supportive action may have been malicious in part. This implicitly Aristotelian perspective is reflected in Marlow's ironic comment that "mediocrity is our mark."[27] Marlow does not conclusively judge Powell's action but instead emphasizes how one might make such a judgment. Powell Sr. is "but a man," incapable of pure good or evil but something more challenging between the two poles – that is, in the archaic sense of the word, a "mediocre" position.

This isn't to say that the doctrine of the mean is a rule that one can simply apply to sort out or evaluate right action. Marlow's use of the word "mediocrity" – a potentially pejorative word – teaches scepticism about the doctrine of the mean. He is wary of the deeply ironic possibility of perverting any ethical system or code through a kind of perfectionism.[28] We see this especially in Marlow's analysis of the Fynes, his summertime neighbours. In the *Nicomachean Ethics* Aristotle explains that the virtuous person's feelings have been habituated to right action – so that the person eventually takes pleasure in the very activities that further happiness given the nature of the human species.[29] The virtuous person is coherent, taking pleasure in what one rationally knows is a specifically human good. However, the Fynes – as Marlow describes them – embody the risks of a too-conscious adoption of what Aristotle intended only as an "outline" for ethical action. Marlow is less interested in a purely "harmonious," integrated character than he is in those who preserve a degree of mystery – where there seem to exist unknown depths, elements that escape apparent or conventional goodness. He is wary of the Fyne family as an example of "the usual unshaded crudity of average people. There was nothing in them that the lamplight might not touch without the slightest risk of indiscretion."[30] Following Marlow's metaphor, the unremarkable majority are "unshaded" or opaque – transparent and uninteresting because they are unhaunted by "shades" or shadows where uncertain or darker motives may lie.

Marlow's scepticism teaches that the idea of virtue risks producing a sterile thus unrealistic form of goodness. We see this critique of a duty-bound ethics – action as a matter of principle – in Marlow's analysis of John Fyne's marriage, and in his outlook on young Powell Jr.'s strict preoccupation with his duties aboard the *Ferndale*. Fyne anxiously focuses on maintaining harmony in his marriage, feeling that disagreement with Zoë would be disastrous.[31] Marlow explains that this usually means Fyne will passively agree with his wife, "endorsing it all as became a good, convinced, husband."[32] Reviling this kind of moral complacency is Conrad's friend and collaborator Ford Madox Ford who writes of the "Englishman [who] must never think; [for] once he does that, he is lost, socially speaking. And he is lost mentally, too [...] His business is to act in conformity with his standard that he learnt at Harrow and Oxford – or at Stepney Board School and a coal mine."[33] A person of any social class, in other words, may end up an unthinking conformist. This dull goodness extends to the Fyne children who somehow manage to play without playfulness. Just as the Fyne marriage is "happy [...] in an earnest, unplayful fashion," the children "romped [...] unplayfully."[34] Marlow is not advocating extreme individualism: we know this when he criticizes Flora's "recklessness" and suggests that "some regard for others should stand in the way of one's playing with danger."[35] Marlow uses the moderate word "some" to advocate duty to – or "regard" for – others: principles, duties, rules of conduct should indeed inform one's actions but rules in themselves are not a sufficient guide to action, because they alone cannot prepare us to respond to chance.

The Ruthless Theorist

If Marlow suggests that consequentialism is an unsatisfactory framework for deliberating about and taking action, his remarks to and about Zoë Fyne show a paradoxical scepticism about philosophy and theory. For example, when John Fyne tells Marlow that Zoë "had formed a very favourable opinion of [Marlow's] practical sagacity,"[36] and that she wants Marlow's help in sorting out what to do about her brother's romantic entanglement with Flora, Marlow rejects the compliment, claiming that "one man's sagacity is much like any other man's sagacity."[37] Although Marlow agrees to discuss Flora with the Fynes over tea at his cottage, much of the conversation entails an effort to dissuade Zoë of her belief that he possesses wisdom of any sort. In fact, Marlow repeats "practical sagacity" so often in his retrospective narrative – the word "sagacity" appears ten times in one chapter – that the term becomes an object of mockery; with each articulation of the harsh-sounding word, especially when paired with "practical," the repeated, internally rhyming "a" flattens the phrase itself as if to reveal its emptiness. This antipathy to the potentially homogenizing effect of practical reason recalls Nietzsche's contempt for virtue as deadening repetition and a consequently mechanistic response to the world.[38] However, Mrs. Fyne's account of Marlow's character is not wrong – for his comments recall Aristotle's doctrine of the mean on various occasions. An obvious example would be his claim that "intelligence leads people astray as far as passion sometimes"; another would be his claim that "one may die of too much endurance as well as too little of it."[39] And the narrator situates Marlow's life between the "unchangeable, safe sea sheltering man from all passions, except its own anger" (a place of reason and spiritedness) and land as a place of changeable emotions and desires.[40] Martin Ray notes Marlow's situation between extremes, arguing that Conrad's character-narrator "must mediate and adjudicate between the tales he hears [in *Chance*], balancing the opposing claims of land and sea, male and female, young and old."[41] Marlow brings back to shore his nurtured capacity for deliberation, a practice that, as Aristotle points out, develops through experience over time.[42] Marlow's seemingly contradictory, overtly contrary response to Mrs. Fyne's compliment invites us to think through the difference between Marlow's penchant for general ideas and Zoë Fyne's theoretical activity.

We learn about Mrs. Fyne's doctrine in the aftermath of Flora's disappearance, before the Fynes receive the letter telling of Flora's elopement with Captain Anthony, when suicide appears to be a real possibility given Marlow's initial meeting with Flora walking dangerously along a precipice.[43] When Marlow wonders if Flora would do such violence to those who care about her, and asks Mrs. Fyne "'if she does not think it was a sort of duty to show elementary consideration, not only for the natural feelings, but even for the prejudices of one's fellow-creatures,'" he is shocked by Mrs. Fyne's response: Flora is exempt from such a duty simply because she is a woman.[44] Despite his shock, Marlow allows that his understanding of Zoë's point of view will always be incomplete, commenting that "I think that she herself did not enlighten me fully. There must have been things not fit for a man to hear."[45] He summarizes what she has shared with him, which is that "no consideration, no delicacy, no tenderness, no scruples should stand in the way of a woman (who by the mere fact of her sex was the predestined victim of conditions created by men's selfish passions, their views, and their abominable tyranny) from taking the shortest cut towards securing for herself the easiest possible existence. She even had the right to go out of existence since some women's existences were made impossible by the short-sighted baseness of men."[46] Mrs. Fyne argues that all women are always already victims, fated to suffer given the tyrannical nature, the "selfish passions," the "baseness" of men; but some women are unfortunately more oppressed than others, making their lives "impossible," left with only one form of agency – that of suicide. True to her name, Zoë attributes male oppressors and female oppression to nature – as if "existence" is in truth mere "existence," inescapably defined by biological "facts." Finding Mrs. Fyne's views extreme, Marlow stutters in response: "No consideration ... Well, I hope you like it."[47] Here we witness something of Aristotle's assertion that the true function of *logos* or speech is not for the sake of communicating information or for the expression or constitution of identity, but "*logos* rather makes it possible for us to discover through deliberation the kinds of goals in terms of which we can best organize our lives – those means which for us constitute human happiness."[48] *Chance* takes this notion further by being considerably less purposive, certain, and conclusive than even the most literary, performative philosophical discourse. In any case, Marlow's shock expresses surprise at Zoë Fyne's harshly reductive outlook on life as zoë. Perhaps Marlow's outlook must allow for this; he may need to recall Jim's situation aboard the *Patna*, and consider Falk's limit case of transgression under extreme duress. These cases remind us that there are conditions of pure pathos, where our actions are beyond judgment – where any action, rather than a right or noble action, is the only option.[49]

Even so, Marlow's response to Mrs. Fyne's doctrine implies, with Aristotle, the uselessness and danger of any inflexible theory or principle, especially when it comes to unexpected situations.[50] Marlow does not trust Mrs. Fyne's claim that Flora's letter, one that Marlow never has the chance to read himself, indicates nothing about an engagement. He does not trust her to read the letter perceptively because "her inexperience might have led her astray. There was no fathoming the innocence of a woman like Mrs. Fyne who, venturing as far as possible in theory, would know nothing of the real aspect of things."[51] Again, Mrs. Fyne tends to push ideas to an extreme. Marlow speaks frankly to Mr. Fyne:

> "The doctrine which I imagine she stuffs into the pretty heads of your girl-guests is almost vengeful. A sort of moral fire-and-sword doctrine [...] it is a mere intellectual exercise. What I see is that in dealing with reality Mrs. Fyne ceases to be tolerant. In other words, that she can't forgive Miss de Barral for being a woman and behaving like a woman. And yet this is not only reasonable and natural, but it is her only chance. A woman against the world has no resources but in herself. Her only means of action is to be what *she is*."[52]

Marlow's language draws out the ironic inflexibility of Mrs. Fyne's doctrine. Her response to Flora exposes the moral vacuity of her theory: it is all abstraction, a "mere intellectual exercise." If Zoë Fyne were to follow her own doctrine – where, again, women are permitted any action to survive, given their subjugation "by mere fact of [their sex]," to the natural and escapable "short-sighted baseness of men," she would not interfere in, or "stand in the way" of, Flora's romance with Captain Anthony. Marlow ironically draws out the implications of Zoë Fyne's theory – that "a woman against the world" can do nothing except "be what she *is*" – to uncover her hypocrisy, and to suggest the hypocrisy that any ideology will risk. In Marlow's view, Zoë Fyne's theory paradoxically covers over an intolerance of the human nature it claims to acknowledge. Marlow's thinking works in the opposite direction: he responds to flesh-and-blood people before him and derives his insights from experience.

The narrative's philosophical integrity, however, lies in the irony of Marlow's critique. Here we see a minimal difference between author and avatar, Conrad and Marlow. Somewhat detracting from Marlow's authority to speak about Mrs. Fyne and Flora, especially considering the novel's Aristotelian affirmation of experience as the foundation of genuine knowledge, is the fact that Marlow – the seaman and perpetual bachelor – has little experience of women. This inexperience may lead Marlow to construct problematic theories about a specifically female nature, and to criticize Mrs. Fyne for "not want[ing] women to be women."[53] That said, the fact that Marlow's claims come to us through frame narrator with whom he is in conversation indicates that his theory is open to amendment. By contrast, Mrs. Fyne takes refuge from life in arguments.[54] Given that experience is mutable and various, ideas informed by experience will be open to amendment also: and so, despite Marlow's crusty misogyny, he leaves open or undefined the question of what a woman "*is*."

If Aristotle teaches that "nature, or biological inheritance, [is] neither wholly determinative of human action nor irrelevant to it," Marlow's outlook approaches this moderate view – as he makes clear in his analysis of the possible roots of Zoë Fyne's doctrine. Marlow emphasizes the shaping forces of habit which, again with Aristotle, considers nature "as a source of problems to be solved and capacities to and inclinations to be shaped."[55] His sceptical yet compassionate, imaginative interest in human character and action gives him a broad yet rich context for understanding Mrs. Fyne's formulation. With characteristic irony, Marlow calls her a "ruthless theorist"[56] and her father Carleon Anthony, a "savage sentimentalist," suggesting that her doctrine is deeply complicit in the outlook that it seems to contest.[57] Marlow

considers its possible roots in the trauma she suffered from her tyrannical poet-father. Perhaps "she had adopted that cool, detached manner to meet her gifted father's outbreaks of selfish temper. It had now
become a second nature."[58] Explaining that Anthony Sr. was "arbitrary
and exacting with his dependents, but marvelously suave in his manner
to admiring strangers," Marlow empathetically imagines the Anthony
children – Zoë and Roderick – suffering through this difference between
external perceptions of the poet and the internal reality at home: "These
contrasted displays must have been particularly exasperating to his
long-suffering family."[59] Contained here is the idea that character is
forged by habit. Aristotle teaches that habit nurtures by way of repetition our potential virtues which become "second nature." Marriage
to John Fyne, although initially an escape from bondage to her father,
leaves Zoë's second or acquired nature and formative circumstances
intact. Mr. Fyne perpetuates the gap between Carleon's domestic and
public lives by taking obvious pride in his wife's parentage: Marlow
remarks that Fyne refers to Carleon Anthony "the poet – you know" at
every opportunity.[60] Although Marlow does not overtly connect Fyne's
snobbish reverence for his late father-in-law and his wife's oppression
(including the ideology that springs from it), Marlow implies that Zoë's
marriage does not exactly free her from the past.

Mrs. Fyne's experience of victimhood may explain her feminist
project, but they do not exempt her from judgment. Her doctrine feels
dangerous – an idea that justifies, and possibly encourages, suicide in
her protégés while concealing petty selfishness and control.[61] Recalling his analysis of Powell Sr.'s possibly malicious intentions behind an
apparent attempt to help the younger Powell, Marlow considers the
possible, deleterious source of Mrs. Fyne's efforts to stop her brother's
romance with Flora:

> her leading idea appeared to me to be not to keep, not to preserve her
> brother, but to get rid of him definitely [...] She wanted the protest to be
> made, emphatically, with Fyne's fullest concurrence in order to make all
> intercourse for the future impossible. Such an action would estrange the
> pair for ever [sic] from the Fynes! She understood her brother and the girl
> too. Happy together, they would never forgive that outspoken hostility –
> and should the marriage turn out badly.... Well, it would be just the same.
> Neither of them would be likely to bring their troubles to such a good
> prophet of evil.
>
> Yes, that must have been her motive. The inspiration of a possibly
> unconscious Machiavellianism! Either she was afraid of having a sister-
> in-law to look after during the husband's long absences; or dreaded the

more or less distant eventuality of her brother being persuaded to leave
the sea [...] bringing to her very door this undesirable, this embarrassing connection. She wanted to be done with it – maybe simply from
the fatigue of continuous effort in good or evil which, in the bulk of
common mortals, accounts for so many surprising inconsistencies of
conduct.[62]

The simplicity of Marlow's earlier assertion that "generally speaking,
an unselfish action is a moral action"[63] is soon complicated his own
insights into Mrs. Fyne's duplicity. Although she claims to be protecting her brother, Mrs. Fyne is in fact – whether she is aware of it or
not – protecting herself; her character suggests that people can appear
and perhaps even feel themselves selflessly preoccupied with another's
happiness while serving their own interests and masking their own less
admirable qualities, such as a prioritization of social reputation over
love, or a willingness to sacrifice others to their own convenience. Any
idée fixe precludes ongoing self-evaluation or self-awareness, at best;
at worst, it may mask the extreme selfishness that, on the surface, it
claims to see and reject. Zoë Fyne embodies Conrad's famous critique
of abstractions: "theory is a cold and lying tombstone of departed truth
(for truth is no more immortal than any other illusion)."[64] Ten years
after writing this pithy epithet, Conrad writes in jest, sounding rather
like Marlow: "I don't know what my philosophy is. I wasn't even aware
I had it. Am sorry to think I must have since you say so. Shall I die of it
do you think?"[65] Philosophy risks becoming a static thus deadly imposition of ideas on vibrant experience. The potentially deleterious effects of
philosophy, defined in antiquity by a necessary, higher, rational separa-
tion from the mutability of everyday life – of experience – are especially
pronounced in Conrad's *Victory* (1915), where we meet the wandering
Axel Heyst who, following his philosopher-father, intentionally dis-
engages from the world of action. The narrator compares Heyst Sr.'s
philosophical outlook to "pitiless cold blasts."[66] Abstraction is purely
rational, which we usually consider in tension with compassion – and
yet, Conrad's critique of cold reason does not advocate its opposite.

Just as there are different ways of practicing theory, there are different ways of dismissing or rejecting it. We know, for example, that both
John Fyne and Charles Powell are suspicious of general ideas – but
the nature of their suspicion is different. Again, Conrad invites us to
make careful and thoughtful distinctions. In John Fyne's case, "general
ideas were not to his taste"[67] – that is, a resistance to general ideas is
implicitly linked to imperceptiveness, to his literally and figuratively
"pedestrian" character. Here, as in Aristotle's "peripatetic" Lyceum,

thinking is bound up with walking. Much like Hermann who relies on the domestic safety of the *Diana*, Fyne intentionally keeps to the paths, suggesting safe because predictable and repetitive thinking: "He was very unobservant except as to the peculiarities of footpaths, on which he was an authority."[68] To know such limited terrain so thoroughly may have its virtues, but such extreme familiarity can limit the imagination, perception, and the ability to construct new ideas. As we shall see, Powell Jr.'s resistance to philosophy is different: it is akin to Marlow's preference for ideas that are open to change because they are open to experience. Marlow prefers to wander – a word that sounds much like "wonder" – an indication of his flexible, contemplative mind.

"Alive to the Slightest Shade of Tone": Seeing, Hearing, and Reading

Recalling how he felt after acquiring his first post, Powell reflects on how an individual's emotions can affect one's sense of others: "Funny how it affects you to be in a peculiar state of mind: everybody that does not act up to your excitement seems so confoundedly unfriendly."[69] Powell's remark implies a critique of emotions – that, unless tempered by reason, they may lead to errors in judgment; but his recollection also implies that for many people, time and memory may be the only means of acquiring some rational, reflective distance from the self. He tells Marlow about a similar experience when first mate Mr. Franklin asked Powell whether he noticed that Captain Anthony seemed "affected" by the fact that his original second mate had broken his collarbone and arm. In response, Powell admitted that he "could not remember any signs of visible grief [...] that owing to the suddenness of this lucky chance coming to him, he was not in a condition to notice the state of other people."[70] Both examples underline the challenge of seeing past one's own affective states and circumstances – but the difficulty also emphasizes the capacity to see as an admirable quality of character that may be developed over time. Marlow's paraphrase of Powell's words – "to notice the state of other people" – reveals the ethical core of perceptiveness.

The novel delves into the potential psychological barriers "to notic[ing] the state of other people," while suggesting that happiness often depends on such powers of observation. Flora and Anthony's unreflective approach to their feelings and beliefs leads them to misinterpret each other's signs and signals. Anthony is vulnerable to Fyne's claims about Flora's motivations because, "having himself always said exactly what he meant he imagined that people (unless they were liars, which of course his brother-in-law could not be) never said more than they meant."[71] Anthony expects the world to match his sense of self as a straightforward person; his lack of scepticism prevents him from addressing Flora directly and candidly about her reticence. Similarly, Flora "could not help believing what she had been told [by her nanny]; that she was in some mysterious way odious and unlovable. It was cruelly true – *to her*."[72] And so, Flora sees Anthony's reticence through the lens of her upbringing – which leads her to misinterpret Anthony's reticence as a mere confirmation that she is indeed essentially unlovable. Marlow uses the metaphor of reading to describe Flora's interpretation of Anthony's facial expressions: "She tried to read something in his face, in that energetic kindly face to which she had become accustomed so soon. But she was not yet capable of understanding its expression. Scared, discouraged on the threshold of adolescence, plunged in a moral misery of the bitterest kind, she had not learned to read – not that sort of language."[73] Marlow suggests that the familiarity of Anthony's face is an impediment; Flora has become "accustomed" to his face too quickly ("so soon") – which may ironically work against her effort to "read" or perceive the nuances of its "expression."[74] A genuine attunement to the other would require more time, and – Marlow implies – more experience and intelligence. Moreover, her youth and inexperience leave her isolated – in a state of "moral misery." She is too innocent, only "on the threshold of adolescence" to register "that sort of language," the language of sexual desire.

Anthony and Flora's marital happiness is finally made possible not by chance, exactly, but by Powell Jr.'s developing, responsive perception of chance or those departures from the routine aboard the *Ferndale*. Marlow's critique of Powell Jr.'s preoccupation with duty aboard the *Ferndale* is an excellent example of an Aristotelian focus on character rather than a strict adherence to rules: "how I feared that Mr. Powell's want of experience would stand in his way of appreciating the unusual [...] I may well have doubted the capacity of a young man too much concerned with the creditable performance of his professional duties to observe what in the nature of things is not easily observable in itself, and still less so under the special circumstances."[75] "Experience" educates one's character: whereas a sailor must of course fulfil his or her duties, the experienced sailor can do so while noticing what falls between or beneath routine activities. Powell's youth made him susceptible to adhering to rules of conduct so closely that they might prevent him from seeing "what in the nature of things is not easily observable in itself." As Julia Annas explains, "Aristotelian habituation is not routine. We learn to be virtuous as we learn to build, and a builder had better not build routinely. As we learn to build, or to be brave, better, we learn to respond ever more intelligently to fresh situations; skill is lost if it degenerates into routine."[76] Mindlessly following a principle or rule involves a basic kind of mimicry devoid of the deeper pleasures of mimesis. A person who copies without any cognitive engagement is involved in a superficial activity that precludes the character-shaping experiences of deliberating and choosing. Aristotelian habituation is character-forming because it engages an agent's cognitive faculties; a person is changed by genuine learning.

The novel suggests that genuine learning involves differentiating between seeing and merely looking. *The Ferndale* initiates an awareness of this difference in Powell. Marlow describes Powell's youthful self, "much slenderer than our robust friend is now, with the bloom of innocence not quite rubbed off his smooth cheeks and apt not only to be interested but also to be surprised by the experience life was holding in store for him."[77] Celebrated here is the liberating potential of "unsophisticated" youth: "Powell, who had sailed out of London all his young seaman's life, told me that it was then, in a moment of entranced vision an hour or so after sunrise, that the river was revealed to him for all time, like a fair face often seen before, which is suddenly perceived to be the expression of an inner and unsuspected beauty, of that something unique and only its own which rouses a passion of wonder and fidelity and an unappeasable memory of its charm."[78] Powell's moment of "entranced" vision is not merely aesthetic – for the familiar "face" of the river was always "fair." The depth of this experience is reflected in Marlow's language: "the river was revealed to [Powell] for all time"; Powell witnesses "that something." He sees the unnameable point at which universality and singularity intersect: "the river is revealed to him for all time" and yet he sees in it what is "unique and only its own." This is the "passion of wonder" itself – that which keeps us "alive to the slightest shade of tone" – perceptive and open to what may not be readily apparent and what may not conform to settled preconceptions, beliefs, and opinions.[79]

In *Chance* reading books becomes a metaphor for observing and perceiving reality. After two unsettling conversations about the captain, first with de Barral and then with Mr. Franklin, both of whom remark that Captain Anthony appears unwell, "Mr. Powell thought that this talk was all nonsense. But his curiosity was awakened [...] Mr. Powell went to his room where he tried to read a book he had already read a good many times."[80] The difficulty reflects a subtle change in Powell: his inability to return to familiar reading habits anticipates his decision to break the rules. Powell sneaks a look into the skylight above the captain's berth on the night – and witnesses de Barral poisoning the captain's drink. The skylight's stained glass, showing Liverpool's coat of arms, had accidentally smashed:

> Mr. Franklin had set the carpenter to patch up the damage with some pieces of plain glass [...] Clear glass. And of course I was not thinking of it. I just stooped to pick up that rope and found my head within three inches of that clear glass and – dash it all! I found myself out. Not half an hour before I was saying to myself that it was impossible to tell what was in people's heads or at the back of their talk, or what they were likely to be up to. And here I found myself up to as low a trick as you can well think of. For, after I had stooped, there I remained prying, spying, anyway looking, where I had no business to look. Not consciously at first, may be.[81]

The motto on the coat of arms is from Virgil, reading *"Deus Nobis Haec Otia Fecit*, "God has bestowed these blessings upon us" – an ironic allusion to a god-ordained universe, given the displacement of the inscribed glass with a colourless window. The actions of men, not gods, inadvertently "bestow [the] bless[ed]" glass that allows Powell to witness and expose de Barral's plot against Captain Anthony. Powell's emphasis on the "clear glass" speaks to his ability to see plainly – free from the "colours" of emotions. Not especially subtle, Powell is "an industrious reader":[82] he can make only the general subject of the captain's book (a history of some kind);[83] but his unprofessional conduct heightens his awareness, "for it can't be denied that our wits are much more alert when engaged in wrong-doing (in which one mustn't be found out) than in righteous occupation."[84] The youth perseveres in his ironically right "wrong-doing" – both physically and literally "stooping" or lowering himself – long enough to glimpse de Barral's hand melodramatically appear between the curtains dividing the cabin, rest above a tumbler, and vanish.

Practical Wisdom Revitalized

Conrad revitalizes practical wisdom in *Chance: A Tale in Two Parts*. Implicitly taking up Aristotle's remark that ethics can only offer an "outline" for contemplating human flourishing or happiness because we live and act in different circumstances and contexts, *Chance* suggests that literary fiction is better suited than philosophy to making us see and appraise character in action in all its rich variety and unpredictability. Marlow reminds us that "practical sagacity" has classical roots: "wisdom tempered by common sense"[85] can be found among "the Seven Sages of Antiquity."[86] The ancient Greeks understood that "common sense" –

knowledge gathered from everyday experience in a shared sphere of action – "tempers" or strengthens and moderates the higher knowledge of universal truths that we call "wisdom." But Marlow brings this insight to life by embodying practical wisdom while refusing its name – wise to the reifying effects of philosophical categories. Instead, Marlow focuses on intrinsic qualities of character, teaching us to admire those with a heightened capacity for perceptiveness. Indeed, the novel suggests that much happiness hangs on one's ability to "interpret aright the signs which experience [...] makes to understanding and emotions."[87] As we have seen, Mrs. Fyne's interpretations are too rigidly informed by theory to be true to life's variations and particularities; Marlow knows that ideas need to be elastic enough to include the unforeseeable: he possesses a higher knowledge of nature and human nature which is that it is wondrously replete with "the unusual," with chance.

A passage from an unpublished manuscript of *Chance* captures the novel's joyous outlook on "the unusual" and the unforeseeable. Marlow contrasts Flora and Anthony's unconventional romance with comparably acceptable "everyday matches," musing that "for most people the pages of life are ruled like the pages of a copybook headed with some sound moral maxim at the top. They can turn them over with the certitude that the very catastrophe shall keep to the traced lines. And it is comforting, in a way, to one's friends and even to oneself to think that one's very misfortunes, if any, will be of the foreseen type."[88] Marlow's account of the copybook life anticipates potentially moralising listeners and readers who would judge Anthony and Flora from the outside, according to commonplace views on marriage; it also contains a related critique of those who seek after and assume the moral comforts of "certitude." Indeed, Marlow observes that many of us live out relatively predictable narratives in "the pages of life" because we are "ruled" by "some sound moral maxim." As his "copybook" metaphor suggests, such lives are directed by some imposed, unquestioned principle that keeps the unforeseeable at bay until "the very catastrophe" of inevitable death. The shadow-side of such repetition must be dreadful conformity – where death looms ever-larger as the only significant "chance" event in a life. The antidote to the copybook – a vehicle for rote learning – is the literary novel which, as a form of art, loves chance; but in leaving the novel unnamed as such – in keeping literary narrative implicit in the copybook's negative example – Marlow's metaphor honours its educational potential while preserving it as a refuge from pedagogical intention or any other subordinating idea. *Chance* is implicitly Aristotelian to the extent that it takes up the philosopher's latent conviction that ethics needs not philosophy but fiction.

Conclusion:
"Speakings"[1]

But every subject in the region of intellect and emotion must have a morality of its own if it is treated at all sincerely; and even the most artful of writers will give himself (and his morality) away in about every third sentence. The varied shades of moral significance which have been discovered in my writings are very numerous. None of them, however, have provoked a hostile manifestation. It may have happened to me to sin against taste now and then, but apparently I have never sinned against the basic feelings and elementary convictions which make life possible to the mass of mankind and, by establishing a standard of judgment, set their idealism free to look for plainer ways, for higher feelings, for deeper purposes.

I cannot say that any particular moral complexion has been put on this novel but I do not think that anybody had detected in it an evil intention. And it is only for their intentions that men can be held responsible. The ultimate effects of whatever they do are far beyond their control. In doing this book my intention was to interest people in my vision of things which is indissolubly allied to the style in which it is expressed. In other words I wanted to write a certain amount of pages in prose, which, strictly speaking, is my proper business [...] I cannot sufficiently insist upon the truth that when I sit down my intentions are always blameless however deplorable the ultimate effect of the act may turn out to be.[2]

How can Conrad claim to work "sincerely" if he also aims to "interest" readers? His point is that an appeal to readers is already built into literature given that its subject is "in the region of intellect and emotion" – just as his outlook is "indissolubly allied to the style in which it is expressed." Conrad acknowledges that readers may impose or "put on" a "moral complexion" rather than work out what he actually "gives away in about every third sentence." After all, a novel's reception exceeds any writer's control once the book is complete and out in the world. Still, as if to remind us that the reading process is neither arbitrary nor wholly relative to the reader's individual perceptions of a given text, he emphasizes the deliberate nature of his craft, repeatedly referring to his "intention" and "intentions." Conrad admits that personal "taste" in all its variety and subjectivity is difficult to anticipate and consistently satisfy; but he defends a deeper achievement, which is to ground his art in "the basic feelings and elementary convictions which make life possible to the mass of mankind and, by establishing a standard of judgment, set their idealism free to look for plainer ways, for higher feelings, for deeper purposes." Conrad urges us to realize that behind and permeating a novel is its intellectual and emotional creator addressing an intellectual and emotional reader. Writing is such a reaching out to a reader; and Conrad assumes that reading is fuelled by the reader's human desire for the unique kind of knowledge that a work of literary fiction contains. A reader wants to know and understand the writer's "vision of things."

This study has attempted to argue that Aristotle casts new light on the crucial importance of "action" in Conrad's "vision of things." In Aristotle's *Poetics*, action is doubly significant, for it refers to the tragic figure's actions and to an idea that unfolds through the elements of a unified or "complete" work of art.[3] The work of tragedy is not radically transformative – a dubious claim for art anyway; rather, it does its work by revealing the grandeur, wonder, and pathos of human beings in action – whether our actions lead to our flourishing or tragically fail to realize happiness. In this light, when Conrad differentiates his own, particular interest in "action [...] nothing but action" from "an endless analysis of affected sentiments," he is defending his interest in writing novels that have an intrinsic end, point, or *telos*.[4] However, we need to go farther to appreciate Conrad's meaning – for one could argue that analysis of emotions may (paradoxically enough) be the anti-teleological *telos* of many novels. Instead, Aristotle helps us see that Conrad's aesthetic and philosophical critique of "endlessness" contains a teleological view of human nature. This outlook is directly apparent in the passage from his memoir *The Mirror of the Sea* that opened this book, where Conrad guides readers to consider that the traditional sailing ship is superior to the steamship. The former is a more fully human environment – a sphere of action that engages the fullest range of a sailor's faculties and potential for action. By contrast, in eliminating "incertitude" as far as possible to fulfil different ends – efficiency, security, productivity, homogeneity – the steamship impoverishes the sailor's seafaring experience. Thus, Conrad is on one level critiquing the shift from sail to steam, but, more deeply, he is contrasting two different dispositions towards nature, including human nature. The endless end of instrumentalism orients the steamer; the traditional sailing ship embodies a different and moderate end of human flourishing because it is open to chance, risk, and accident – the unstable ground of agency. Here, an Aristotelian reading of Conrad paradoxically opens onto twentieth-century philosophical critiques of technology, instrumentalism, and totality – a potential area for further research. Implicit in Conrad's critique is an outlook on art itself as an antidote to the instrumentalism that he feared had taken such a firm hold on humanity in the modern world.

What of Conrad's art, then? Reflecting on the preceding chapters and hoping to inspire better work, I suggest that Conrad's particular use of the word "action" is a key to reading his fiction. "Action" – a preoccupation with character, conduct, and human flourishing – unlocks the formation of the compassionate yet rational narrator as a guide to the reader's judgment in Conrad's *oeuvre* from *An Outcast of the Islands* to *Chance*. Patterns of repetition tie these novels together for the reader. In *An Outcast*, between the unnamed narrator's ironic distance and the classically tragic Captain Lingard, a narrative voice and outlook begin to form as a critical response to the condition of modern pathos that Willems embodies. In *Lord Jim*, Marlow brings together Lingard's compassion and the unnamed narrator's scepticism, just as the novel deepens *An Outcast*'s engagement with the tropes of ancient tragedy to critique modernity. There are myriad continuities between these two works: if Marlow is much like Lingard, Jim is too – borrowing from his classically heroic qualities of character. Moreover, Jim's position as a protégé who transgresses, invites us to contrast his character with Willems. Within each novel the narrator invites us to distinguish between settings, characters, and actions – and together the novels deepen and strengthen this appeal. We come to see that Jim, like Lingard, is worthy of admiration (however qualified), whereas Willems is merely pathetic. Lingard tragically pushes his compassion too far, whereas *Lord Jim*'s Marlow is compassionate yet rational thus a more trustworthy guide. *Falk: A Reminiscence* contains a Marlovian narrator who looks back on a formative period in his youth when he took up his first command. Unlike Jim who dies a classically tragic figure in aristocratic Patusan, the youth in *Falk* facilitates a comedic resolution: he brings into balance public and private goods – his successful command and Falk's marriage to Hermann's niece. This happy resolution hinges on the young captain's compassionate yet rational appraisal of Falk. Both Falk and

Jim are haunted by their transgressions – an idea of a human limit, what we cannot or should not do. Both novels, taken together, look at how we come to terms with transgressions with which we must live or continue to live. The novels, especially when read together, convey Conrad's profoundly moderate realism – his compassionate, clear-eyed judgement whereby we must not, cannot, abandon ethical human limits on our actions. And yet it is incumbent on us to consider conduct in contexts, especially spheres of action shaped by modern indeterminacy.

In *Chance*, also a comedy, Marlow returns to give us a joyous outlook on practical wisdom, what he calls the "science of life" – the capacity to perceive and "seize on" opportunities for happiness. Just as the official inquiry fails Jim, and conventional morality fails Falk, in *Chance* Marlow shows us that consequentialism and modern theory are insufficient frameworks for understanding and appraising character and conduct. Instead, we need knowledge of human nature gathered from experience combined with perceptiveness and a readiness to act. Conrad's discerning narrator and the novels themselves appraise characters according to a "standard of judgement" that is grounded in "elementary" human nature. Given this emphasis on solid ground, when Conrad writes that he intends with his fiction to "set [our] idealism free," the formulation is almost as controversial as Aristotle's discussion of *catharsis* (purgation or education?) in the *Poetics* and *Politics*. If taken out of context, Conrad's phrase might appear to claim for his art the capacity to inspire ideals. However, from what we have seen in this study, at least, the word "idealism" is best read in Conrad's prose as a red flag. With Aristotle's theory of *catharsis* as an education – rather than a purgation or expulsion – of the emotions of pity and terror, so that citizens can return to the *polis* with a renewed sense of what is both necessary and possible in human nature, we can read Conrad's intention to "set [our] idealism free" as a disposition to move us beyond abstract "isms" so that we may, as *Falk*'s Marlovian narrator says, "get in touch with the real actuality at our elbow."[5] If the previous chapters attend in part to Conrad's outlook on abstract ideals as powerful impediments to discernment and to human happiness, here we can advance that in the above passage Conrad is saying that he means to free us from idealism so we can engage in the more challenging pursuit of "plainer ways," "higher feelings," and "deeper purposes."

Aristotle's theory of tragedy helps us recognize that Conrad's discerning narrator is a hopeful response to what he observes to be impoverished spheres of action and the shaping powers of history. *An Outcast*'s unnamed narrator mourns "the old sea" in contrast with the "the sea of to-day"; Captain Lingard's classically heroic character is increasingly pushed to the margins in the Malay trilogy's chronology; an increasingly modernized world will eventually subsume the different, aristocratic world of Patusan; and in *Falk* the sailors long for a lost and distant era of heroism at sea. And yet, Conrad's fiction is replete with characters who are subject to chance, risk, and accident but not reducible to them. Neither gods above "incertitude" nor passive beasts radically determined by it, by nature we exist between those extremes. Even as we are subject to spheres of action and historical forces largely beyond our control, literature offers us a capacious emotional and intellectual refuge from what, as we saw in this study's introduction, Conrad called the conformity of "the public mind."[6] Such a refuge is rich with what Marlow poetically describes as "something unique and only its own" in nature, which includes human nature.[7] Conrad's moderate, impassioned ethic of wonder reminds us that it is possible to see each other and ourselves, if always and necessarily imperfectly. Aristotle paradoxically returns us to Conrad himself – to the immense achievement of his body of work and the pleasures of reading it attentively, on its own terms. To understand Joseph Conrad, we need to read more Joseph Conrad. His morality is not a moral or message or instruction but rather a quality that pervades his fiction, just as an intimate friend's character appears to us in some irreducible, "indissoluble" yet discernible way in their words and gestures. A novel is a human thing – and a writer's work, no matter the distance of time or place, contains the voice of a lifelong friend.

Notes

Introduction: The Deeper Significance of Sailing Ships

1 Joseph Conrad, *The Mirror of the Sea* in *The Mirror of the Sea* and *A Personal Record* (Oxford: Oxford World's Classics, 1988), 30–1.

2 Agathon, qtd. in Aristotle, *Nicomachean Ethics* 1140a20, *Aristotle's Nicomachean Ethics: A New Translation*, trans. Robert C. Bartlett and Susan Collins (Chicago: Chicago University Press, 2012).

3 To Richard Curle, 17 July 1923, qtd. in Eloise Knapp Hay, *The Political Novels of Joseph Conrad: A Critical Study with a New Preface* (Chicago: University of Chicago Press, 1981), 5.

4 I address this continuity in chapter 1.

5 On Nietzsche's roots in Romanticism see Ernst Behler, *German Romantic Literary Theory* (Cambridge: Cambridge University Press, 1993).

6 Agathon, qtd. in Aristotle 1140a20, *Aristotle's Nicomachean Ethics*.

7 "Anything which is incapable of action is incapable of doing anything by chance." Aristotle, *Physics* 197b5, trans. Robin Waterfield (Oxford: Oxford World's Classics, 1996).

8 Terry Eagleton, *Trouble with Strangers : A Study of Ethics* (Sussex: Wiley-Blackwell, 2009), 286.

9 Ibid., 287. In Nietzsche's extremely pessimistic view, tragedy exposes or lays bare painful, inevitable truths (or inevitability as the truth) – the driving force of art as a saving illusion. For Nietzsche, tragedy has no elevating outcome or resolution, as it does for Aristotle, where the audience's painful emotions of pity and fear are transformed or, as Carnes Lord argues, educated. Carnes Lord, *Education and Culture in the Political Thought of Aristotle* (Ithaca: Cornell University Press, 1982).

10 Laurence Davies distinguishes between nihilism and scepticism in "'The Thing Which Was Not' and The Thing That Is Also: Conrad's Ironic Foreshadowing," *Conrad in the Twenty-First Century: Contemporary Approaches and Perspectives* (London: Routledge, 2005), 233.

11 To George T. Keating, 14 December 1922, *Notes on Life and Letters*, II (New York: Doubleday, 1927), 289. Quoted in Eloise Knapp Hay, *The Political Novels of Joseph Conrad*, 15n18.

12 Born on 3 December 1857, in Berdyczów, a Polish city occupied by Russia since 1793, Conrad, with his parents Apollo and Ewa Korzenowski, moved several times – mostly following Apollo's literary and political activities – until 1862 when they were exiled to Vologda, Russia, where his mother died three years later from exhaustion and illness. Conrad and Apollo moved to Kraków in 1869 where Apollo died after a prolonged illness. Apart from some trips to Switzerland and a short stay in a boarding house in Lwów, Kraców was his home until he left for Marseilles to join the French merchant marine. For an exceptionally clear chronology of Conrad's life, see Owen Knowles and Gene M. Moore, *The Oxford Reader's Companion to Conrad* (London: Oxford University Press), xiii–xxxviii.

13 Zdzisław Najder, "Joseph Conrad and the Classical World," *Conrad in Perspective: Essays on Art and Fidelity* (Cambridge: Cambridge University Press, 1997), 29.

14 Jan Woleński, "The Reception of Aristotle in Poland around 1900," *Aristote au XIX Siècle*, Denis Thouard, éd. (Paris: Les Presses Universitaire Septentrion, 2004), 395.

15 A decline in the popularity of Aristotelian ethics can be seen throughout eighteenth-century Europe. See Murray Faure, "Understanding Aristotle's Prudence and its Resurgence in Postmodern Times," *Phronimon* 14, no. 2 (2013): 59.

16 T.A. Sinclair, Translator's Introduction, *Politics*, ed. Trevor J. Saunders (London: Penguin, 1992), 17.

17 Conrad's formal education was quite irregular, due to the instability of his family life and his own ill health. However, Najder includes among Conrad's "intellectual achievements at the time he left home" for Marseilles in 1874, a "tolerably good" knowledge of Latin and German, in addition to "a certain amount of Greek, which was taught with the third form; by the fourth form the *Iliad* was being read [...] He probably knew a good deal of history, particularly that of antiquity." See *Joseph Conrad: A Life*, trans. Halina Najder (New York: Camden House, 2007), 46–7.

18 Aristotle's illustrative examples frequently include sailors.

19 Jeremy Hawthorn, Endnote, Joseph Conrad's *Under Western Eyes* (Oxford: Oxford University Press, 2003), 301n234.

20 Edward Said, "Conrad and Nietzsche," ed. Norman Sherry, *Joseph Conrad* (Palgrave MacMillan, 1976), 66.

21 Eloise Knapp Hay, *The Political Novels of Joseph Conrad* (Chicago: University of Chicago Press, 1963). Avrom Fleishman, *Conrad's Politics: Community and Anarchy in the Fiction of Joseph Conrad* (Baltimore: Johns Hopkins Press, 1967), 77. In "The Ship of State and its Captain in Plato and Conrad," Nic

Panagopoulos argues that we can go deeper than Fleishman to recognize the Platonic underpinnings of Conrad's organicist outlook in *Heart of Darkness*. *The Conradian: The Journal of the Joseph Conrad Society (UK)* 45.1 (Spring 2020), 73–90.

22 David Adams, *Colonial Odysseys: Empire and Epic in the Modernist Novel* (Ithaca: Cornell University Press, 2003). Also see Terence Bowers, "Conrad's *Aeneid*: *Heart of Darkness* and the Classical Epic," *Conradiana: A Journal of Joseph Conrad Studies* 38.2 (Summer 2006): 115–42, and Richard Ambrosini, "Tragic Adventures: Conrad's and Marlow's Conflicting Narratives in *Lord Jim*," *The Conradian: The Journal of the Joseph Conrad Society (UK)* 38.1 (Spring 2013): 53–71.

23 Amar Acharaïou, *Rethinking Post-colonialism: Colonialist Discourse in Modern Literature and the Legacy of Classical Writers* (London: Palgrave Macmillan, 2008).

24 Debra Romanick Baldwin, "Marlow, Socrates, and an Ancient Quarrel in *Chance*," *Centennial Essays on Conrad's Chance*, eds. Alan H. Simmons and Susan Jones (Leiden: Brill, 2016), 53.

25 Nic Panagopoulos, "Conrad's Poetics: An Aristotelian Reading of *Heart of Darkness*," *L'époque Conradienne* 40 (2015–17): 117–49. Panagopoulos's conclusion suggests the Nietzschean framework of his earlier work: "Conrad has Marlow affirm the spoudaois/favlos dichotomy by agreeing with the Russian and insisting, against the evidence, that Kurtz was 'a remarkable man' [... which] indicates a regressive strategy in *Heart of Darkness* which relates to the re/enchanting project of literary Modernism, the idea that a return to myth was the only way to restore meaning, value, and presence to a world that had lost its illusions" (25). See also Panagopoulos's inquiry into the classical roots and significance of the phrase "under a cloud" in *Lord Jim* in "Jim 'Under a Cloud': The Career of a Leitmotif," *Yearbook of Conrad Studies (Poland)* 12 (2017): 59–69.

26 To William Blackwood, 31 May 1902, *Collected Letters of Joseph Conrad, Volume 2: 1898–1902*, eds. Frederick R. Karl and Laurence Davies (Cambridge: Cambridge University. Press, 1986), 418.

27 Jeremy Hawthorn, "Life Sentences: Linearity and Its Discontents in *An Outcast of the Islands*," *Voice, Sequence, History, Genre* (Columbus: University of Ohio Press, 2008), 97.

28 Carol Poster, "Whose Aristotle? Which Aristotelianism? A Historical Prolegomenon to Thomas Farrell's Norms of Rhetorical Culture," *Philosophy and Rhetoric* 41, no. 4 (2008): 376.

29 Ibid. Poster draws on the writings of Scottish scholars James Moor and John Gillies, pointing out that their project extends to the work of twentieth-century intellectuals such as Alasdair MacIntyre and Richard McKeon.

30 Stephen Halliwell, Epilogue, *Aristotle's Poetics*, ed. Amélie Rorty (Princeton: Princeton University Press, 1992), 420.

1 Conrad's Vision of Things

1 To William Blackwood, 31 May 1902, *Collected Letters of Joseph Conrad, Volume 2: 1898–1902*, eds. Frederick R. Karl and Laurence Davies (Cambridge: Cambridge University Press, 1986), 418.
2 Bertrand Russell, *Portraits from Memory and Other Essays* (London: George Allen & Unwin, 1956), 89.
3 Conrad, "Author's Note" (1920), *Chance: A Tale in Two Parts*, ed. Martin Ray (Oxford: Oxford World's Classics, 1988), xxxiv.
4 Derek Attridge, *The Singularity of Literature* (London: Routledge, 2004), 3.
5 Brian Artese, *Testimony on Trial: Conrad, James, and the Contest for Modernism* (Toronto: University of Toronto Press, 2012), 3.
6 Conventional categories of literary history are by no means as simple as my use of the convenient terms "Victorian" and "Edwardian" suggest. Technically, the Victorian era ended in 1901 with the death of the Queen; "Edwardian" marks the reign of King Edward VII from 1901 to 1910. We refer however to "the long nineteenth century" to reflect the primacy of social mores, practices, values, and so on over the literalism of specific dates. I am using the terms as shorthand for a collection of values, attitudes, and cultural practices that extend beyond Queen Victoria and King Edward's reigns until the shattering events of the twentieth century. Similarly, the "modern novel" was beginning to emerge before the technical end of the Victorian era. See Ian Watt, *Conrad in the Nineteenth Century* (Berkeley: University of California Press, 1978).
7 Andrea White provides a useful overview in "Conrad and Modernism," *A Historical Guide to Joseph Conrad*, John Peters ed. (Oxford: Oxford University Press, 2010), 163–96. Also see Con Coroneos, *Space, Conrad, and Modernity* (Oxford: Oxford University Press, 2002); Daphna Erdinast-Vulcan, *Joseph Conrad and the Modern Temper* (Cambridge: Cambridge University Press, 1991) and *The Strange Short Fiction of Joseph Conrad: Writing, Culture, and Subjectivity* (Cambridge: Cambridge University Press, 1999); Kenneth Graham, "Conrad and Modernism," *The Cambridge Companion to Joseph Conrad*, ed. John Stape (Cambridge: Cambridge University Press, 1996), 203–22; Michael Greany, *Conrad, Language, and Narrative* (Cambridge: Cambridge University Press, 2002); Jacob Lothe, Jeremy Hawthorn, James Phelan, eds. *Joseph Conrad: Voice, Sequence, History, Genre* (Columbus: Ohio State University Press, 2008); Josiane Paccaud-Huguet, "'One of those trifles that awaken ideas': The Conradian

Moment," *The Conradian: The Journal of the Joseph Conrad Society (UK)* 31,
no. 1 (Spring 2006): 75–88; Nic Panagopoulos, *The Fiction of Joseph Conrad:
The Influence of Schopenhauer and Nietzsche* (London: Peter Lang, 1998);
David Thorburn, *Conrad's Romanticism* (New Haven: Yale University
Press, 1974); Mark A. Wollaeger, *Joseph Conrad and the Fictions of Skepticism*
(Stanford: Stanford University Press, 1990).

8 David Thorburn, *Conrad's Romanticism*, 161–2.

9 Ibid., 165.

10 Conrad, "Author's Note" (1920), *The Shadow-Line* (Oxford: Oxford
University Press, 2002), 110.

11 Ibid.

12 Daphna Erdinast-Vulcan, *The Strange Short Fiction of Joseph Conrad: Writing,
Culture, and Subjectivity* (Cambridge: Cambridge University Press, 1999), 2–3.

13 Russell, *Portraits from Memory and Other Essays*, 89.

14 Lorraine Clark addresses Conrad's implicit critique of Rousseauvian
compassion in "Rousseau and Political Compassion in *The N[*****] of the
Narcissus*," *Conradiana: A Journal of Joseph Conrad Studies* 31, no. 2 (1999): 120–30.

15 Zdzisław Najder, *Conrad in Perspective: Essays on Art and Fidelity*
(Cambridge: Cambridge University Press, 1997), 144.

16 Conrad, "Author's Note" (1920), *Chance: A Tale in Two Parts* (Oxford:
Oxford World's Classics, 1988), xxxiv.

17 Owen Knowles and Gene M. Moore, *Oxford Reader's Companion to Conrad*
(London: Oxford, 2000), xxxii; 43; 314.

18 To William Blackwood, 31 May 1902, *Collected Letters, Vol. 2*, 418. Conrad is
implying that his turn away from "endless analysis" means a turn towards
shared human experience, to universals; it would be interesting, although
beyond the scope of this study, to think through his allusion to Shylock's
famous rhetorical question: "If you prick us do we not bleed?"

19 Conrad's allusion to Wagner is not unfounded; twelve years later, one
of Conrad's contemporary critics tangentially compares him to Wagner.
See James Huneker, "The Genius of Joseph Conrad," *The North American
Review* 200, no. 705 (August 1914): 271.

20 Conrad's reference to Shylock's famous speech is ambiguous. Is he
referring to a simple interpretation of the claim (about shared humanity);
or is he working with Shylock's ironic intimations about the hypocrisy
of his (Christian) listeners to imply that Blackwood is hypocritically
unforgiving or merciless?

21 In his ironic outlook on the new, Conrad anticipates Jacques Derrida's
own anticipatory engagement with the paradox of newness: "Perhaps the
impossible is the only possible chance of something new, of some new
philosophy of the new." *Politics of Friendship*, trans. George Collins (New
York: Verso, 1997), 36.

22 An Aristotelian reading of Conrad's focus on action and intention draws out the moral significance of Conrad's language. In the *Nicomachean Ethics* 1105a31–4, Aristotle defines virtue as intentional action: the virtuous person "acts knowingly"; "acts by choosing and by choosing the actions in question for their own sake"; and "acts while being in a steady and unwavering state." *Aristotle's Nicomachean Ethics: A New Translation*, trans. Robert C. Bartlett and Susan D. Collins (Chicago: Chicago University Press, 2011).

23 Conrad married Jessie in London on 24 March 1896; that year, he wrote to Garnett on March 23rd or 24th.

24 To Edward Garnett, Monday [23/24 March 1896], *Collected Letters, Vol. 1 (1861–1897)*, eds. Fredrick R. Karl and Laurence Davies (Cambridge: Cambridge University Press), 268.

25 Nietzsche pervaded intellectual and artistic communities in early twentieth century Britain. Two of Conrad's friends and correspondents were working on Nietzschean terrain: R.B. Cunningham Graham, who in 1898 would write for *The Eagle and the Serpent: A Journal of Egoistic Philosophy and Sociology*; and Edward Garnett, who would publish an article on the controversial philosopher in the following year. See Edward Garnett, "Views and Reviews: Nietzsche," *The Outlook* (8 July 1899), 746–8. Conrad is most likely thinking of Nietzsche's critique of metaphysical presence or "being" – as a fiction or illusion that must give way to the deeper, painful truth of perpetual impermanence or "becoming."

26 Conrad could be referring to Nietzsche or Schopenhauer. See "Schopenhauer, Arthur," Knowles and Moore, 365–6.

27 Conrad was first mate aboard *The Torrens* when he met Galsworthy, a passenger, in 1893.

28 To John Galsworthy, 11 February 1899, qtd. in *Henry James: The Critical Heritage*, ed. Roger Gard (London: Routledge, 1982), 271.

29 To William Blackwood, 31 May 1902, *Collected Letters, Vol. 2*, 418.

30 Conrad, qtd. in Hay, *The Political Novels of Joseph Conrad: A Critical Study with a New Preface* (Chicago: University of Chicago Press, 1981), 13.

31 Geoffrey Galt Harpham, *One of Us: The Mastery of Joseph Conrad* (Chicago: University of Chicago Press 1996), 56.

32 To C.K. Scott Moncrieff, 17 December 1922, in *Joseph Conrad: Selected Literary Criticism and The Shadow-Line*, ed. Alan Ingram (New York: Methuen, 1986), 102.

33 Ibid., 103.

34 To Roger Fry, 3 October 1922, *The Letters of Virginia Woolf, Volume 2*, eds. Nigel Nicolson and Joanne Trautmann (New York: Harcourt Brace Jovanovich, 1977), 565.

35 Richard Curle, *The Last Twelve Years of Conrad* (Garden City, NY: Doubleday, Doran and Company, Inc., 1928).
36 Thomas Pfau, *Minding the Modern: Human Agency, Intellectual Traditions, and Responsible Knowledge* (Indiana: University of Notre Dame Press, 2013), 285.
37 David Hume, "Concerning Moral Sentiment," Appendix 1, *An Enquiry Concerning the Principles of Morals*, ed. J.B. Schneewind (Indianapolis: Hackett, 1893), 87.
38 Ibid.
39 Pfau, *Minding the Modern*, 14.
40 Pfau explains that in *Beyond Good and Evil*, Nietzsche "summarily dismisses the concept and word 'will' as nothing more than a popular prejudice [*Volks-Voruteil*] prone to nurture the illusion of a unified, causally efficient, and self-conscious agent [...] Yet for Nietzsche, as previously for Hume, what prompts and licenses this critique is the unexamined assumption that human agency is just another instance of efficient causation, albeit one deluded by supposing itself capable of originating values and, therefore, trapped in the 'error of false causation.'" *Minding the Modern*, 285. While Conrad writes of illusions – the illusions of youth, for example – even just his adherence to an ethics and aesthetics of "action" suggests that his concept/deployment of illusion differs from Nietzsche's, or that the implications of illusion(s) are different for Conrad.
41 Richard Janko, "action," Glossary, Aristotle, *Poetics* (Indianapolis: Hackett, 1987), 196.
42 Aristotle, *Poetics* 50a16–22, trans. Richard Janko (Indianapolis: Hackett, 1987). Emphasis added
43 Aristotle, *Poetics* 49b25–9.
44 Ibid., 51b1.
45 Ibid., 51a31–2.
46 To William Blackwood, 31 December 1898, qtd. in Katherine Isobel Baxter, *Joseph Conrad and the Swan Song of Romance* (Surrey: Ashgate, 2010), 21.
47 This reading offers an alternative to Matthew Paul Carlson's claim that Conrad's emphasis on action rather than individuals means "he is not concerned with the presentation of realized, human characters but with presentation [i.e., what Carlson refers to as "the properties of literary language"] as such." See "Conrad's Early Fiction and the Aesthetic of Dehumanization," *The Conradian: The Journal of the Joseph Conrad Society (UK)* 36, no. 1 (Spring 2011): 21; 14.
     Conrad's emphasis on action (and character and representation) is in tension with how his fiction registers a modern concern with presentation or language as language.
48 Conrad, *A Personal Record*, eds. Zdzisław Najder and J.H. Stape (Cambridge: Cambridge University Press, 2008), 27–8.

49　Stephen Halliwell argues that the *Poetics* "should be seen above all
as a serious response to Plato's devaluation of poetic 'falsehood': Ar.
restores poetry's respectability by recognizing that its fictions can,
through the preferably dramatic presentation of action and character,
entail significance which has a kinship with the mode of understanding
employed by the philosopher (who, for Ar. as for Plato, has supreme
access to truth and wisdom)." Commentary, *The Poetics of Aristotle*
(Chapel Hill: University of North Carolina Press, 1987), 109. This
argument is reinforced by Ryan Drake who argues that both pleasure and
understanding are given equal weight in Aristotle's account of the *telos*
of tragedy in the *Poetics*. See "Wonder, Nature and the Ends of Tragedy,"
International Philosophical Quarterly 50, no. 1 (March 2010): 77–91.

50　Aristotle, *Poetics* 51b7–10.

51　Carnes Lord, *Education and Culture in the Political Thought of Aristotle*
(Ithaca: Cornell University Press, 1982), 18–19. Emphasis added

52　"Since a poet represents, just like a painter or some other maker of
images, at any moment he is necessarily representing one of three things,
either (a) things as they were or are or (b) things as people say and think
[they were or are], or (c) things as they should be." Aristotle, *Poetics*
60b8–11.

53　Conrad, Preface to *The N[*****] of the "Narcissus": A Tale of the Sea* in *The
N[*****] of the "Narcissus," Typhoon, The Shadow-Line* (London: J.M. Dent &
Sons Ltd., 1945), 5.

54　This implicit concern to defend art's respite from or challenge to an
economy of exchange, including what Conrad implies is a dominant
economic, use-value perspective on human activity anticipates Derrida's
deconstruction of the gift, especially in *Given Time 1: Counterfeit Money*,
trans. Peggy Kamuf (Chicago: University of Chicago Press, 1992) and
The Gift of Death, trans. David Wills (Chicago: University of Chicago
Press, 1995).

55　Conrad, Preface to *The N[*****] of the "Narcissus": A Tale of the Sea*, 6.
Emphasis added

2 *An Outcast of the Islands*: Tragedy, Pathos, and Conrad's Narrative Appeal

1　Joseph Conrad, *An Outcast of the Islands* (Cambridge: Cambridge
University Press, 2016), 20.

2　In 1896 Conrad began working on *The Rescue* (which he originally
intended to be a short story); in 1916 he returned to the project in earnest.
See Owen Knowles and Gene Moore, *Oxford Reader's Companion* (Oxford:
Oxford University Press, 2000), 245.

3 Michael Valdez Moses, *The Novel and the Globalization of Culture* (Oxford: Oxford University Press, 1995), xiv.

4 Allan Simmons, *Joseph Conrad* (New York: Palgrave Macmillan, 2006), 212.

5 Terry Eagleton, *Trouble with Strangers: A Study of Ethics* (London: Wiley Blackwell: 2008), 286.

6 Eagleton, *Sweet Violence: The Idea of the Tragic* (Oxford: Wiley, 2003), 55.

7 David Gallop, "Jane Austen and the Aristotelian Ethic," *Philosophy and Literature* 23, no. 1 (1999): 96–109.

8 Conrad, *An Outcast*, 149.

9 Leonard Orr, "*Almayer's Folly* (1895) and *An Outcast of the Islands* (1896)," *A Joseph Conrad Companion*, eds. Leonard Orr and Theodore Billy (Westport, CT: Greenwood Press, 1999), 37; Claude Maisonnat, "The Returns of the Reader in *An Outcast of the Islands*," *Yearbook of Conrad Studies* 3 (2007): 76.

10 Aristotle, *Poetics* 53a11–12, trans. Richard Janko (Indianapolis: Hackett, 1987).

11 See Aristide Tessitore who points out that for Aristotle "the failure to develop one's capacities for both reason and excellence precludes the possibility of lasting happiness notwithstanding the many advantages that turn upon wealth, good birth, status, and power." *Reading Aristotle's* Ethics: *Virtue, Rhetoric, and Political Philosophy* (Albany: SUNY Press, 1996), 22.

12 Aristotle, *Poetics* 53a9–10.

13 Conrad, *An Outcast*, 23.

14 Ibid.

15 Ibid.

16 Ibid.

17 Ibid., 21.

18 Ibid., 42.

19 Ibid.

20 Ibid., 41.

21 The narrative ironically juxtaposes Lingard's request that Willems trust him; his declaration that Willems could be trusted with the location of the "secret river"; and Willems's untrustworthiness: "While Lingard spoke [about his trading post] Willems looked up quickly but soon his head fell on his breast in the discouraging certitude that the knowledge he and Hudig had wished for so much had come to him too late. He sat in a listless attitude" (42).

22 Conrad, *An Outcast*, 41.

23 Ibid., 15.

24 Ibid.

25 Ibid.

26 Ibid., 17.

27 Aristotle, *Poetics* 49a36–7.

28 J.H. Stape, Introduction to *An Outcast of the Islands* (Oxford: Oxford World's Classics, 1992), xi.
29 Conrad, *An Outcast*, 16.
30 Ibid.
31 Ibid., 15.
32 Conrad distinguishes between hollow authority or power that historical accident may confer (such as being born white when whiteness is ideologically inscribed with superiority), and real authority grounded in character and action, such as Lingard embodies. But he also shows an ironical appropriation of European racism – where whiteness can be inscribed by an embarrassing idiocy (such as Willems embodies when he holds court at the billiards club).
33 Conrad, *An Outcast*.
34 Ibid., 78.
35 Conrad made several disparaging comments about Nietzsche as a philosopher of extremes in his correspondence. See Conrad's letter to Helen Sanderson, July 1899, *Collected Letters of Joseph Conrad, Volume 2: 1898–1902*, eds. Frederick R. Karl and Laurence Davies (Cambridge: Cambridge University Press, 1896), and his essay, "The Crime of Partition" (originally published in the *Fortnightly Review*, May 1919). For a succinct analysis of Conrad's critique of Nietzsche's "barbarism and cruelty" see John Wylie Griffith's *Conrad and the Anthropological Dilemma: "bewildered traveler"* (Oxford: Clarendon Press, 1995), 193–4.
36 Friedrich Nietzsche, *The Birth of Tragedy*, The Birth of Tragedy and the Case of Wagner, trans. Walter Kauffman (New York: Vintage Books, 1967), 31–151.
37 Conrad, *An Outcast*, 13.
38 Aristotle, *Politics* 1325a16, trans. T.A. Sinclair (London: Penguin, 1962).
39 Aristotle, *Nicomachean Ethics* 1103b22–6, *Aristotle's Nicomachean Ethics: A New Translation*, trans. Robert C. Bartlett and Susan D. Collins (Chicago: University of Chicago Press, 2011).
40 Conrad, *An Outcast*, 18.
41 Ibid., 13.
42 Agathon, qtd. in Aristotle, *Nicomachean Ethics* 1139b10–11.
43 Aristotle, *Poetics* 52a25.
44 Conrad, *An Outcast*, 59.
45 Ibid., 13.
46 Thus, the novel suggests that an ethics of overcoming – or of the will – does not affirm, but is hostile, to life itself.
47 Conrad, *An Outcast*, 66–7. Willems might be read as an embodiment of a Nietzschean critique of teleological ethics – of an ethics that is literally driven towards the ultimate end of death. See David Roochnik's reading of "the strangeness" of life's teleological structure in "Teleology as death

wish: a Nietzschean critique of Aristotle," 7 February 2014, St. John's
College, Annapolis, MD, mp3, 59:07, https://digitalarchives.sjc.edu
/items/show/52.

48 Ibid., 69. Emphasis added.

49 Ibid., 70.

50 Ibid., 105. Emphasis added.

51 Nietzsche, "On Redemption," *Thus Spake Zarathustra: A Book for Everyone
    and Nobody*, trans. Graham Parkes (London: Penguin, 2005), 121.

52 Conrad, *An Outcast*, 105.

53 Aristotle, *Poetics* 52a30–1.

54 Halliwell, *Aristotle's* Poetics (Chapel Hill: University of North Carolina
    Press, 1986), 318.

55 As Halliwell puts it, "Reversal (*peripeteia*) and recognition (*anagnōrisis*,
    sometimes translated as 'discovery') are closely linked not just in Ar.s'
    theory but in their essential implications for tragedy. Both are devices
    that focus and concentrate a tragic transformation in dramatic moments
    of ironic or paradoxical force. Reversal [...] presupposes, just as does
    recognition, a significant element of ignorance at work in the dramatic
    situation." Commentary, *The Poetics of Aristotle* (Chapel Hill: University of
    North Carolina Press, 1987), 116.

56 Conrad, *An Outcast*, 15.

57 Ibid., 28.

58 John D. Caputo explains that "non-knowing puts faith and passion to the
    test, stretching them beyond the too limited expectations that knowledge
    tolerates. Derrida does not propose a learned unknowing, which is but a
    more oblique and negative way to know something still higher [...] but a
    lover's unknowing [...] which keeps the future open by [...] its messianic
    yearning for what is "to come." *The Prayers and Tears of Jacques Derrida:
    Religion without Religion* (Indiana: Indiana University Press, 1997), 103.

59 Translators Bartlett and Collins note that Aristotle's phrase *ho logos* "may
    well refer to 'correct reason.'"*Aristotle's* Nicomachean Ethics 2n9. The
    adjective "correct" implies the possibility of "incorrect" – i.e., a possible
    misuse of reason. See also Aristotle on the dangers of "seeking refuge in
    argument." *Nicomachean Ethics* 1105b13–14.

60 Conrad, *An Outcast*, 33.

61 Ibid., 34.

62 Stape, Introduction, x.

63 Conrad, *An Outcast*, 267.

64 This opening onto the new – a suggestion of hope – might be dialectical
    thus Hegelian-Nietzschean: between Lingard (ancient) and Willems
    (modern) there emerges a return of the "ethical substance" with a
    difference.

65 Conrad, *An Outcast*, 211.

66 Ibid.

67 Ibid., 210.

68 Aristotle famously writes that "it was because of wonder that men both now and originally began to philosophize." Aristotle, *Metaphysics*, trans. H.C. Lawson-Tancred (London: Penguin, 2004), 9.

69 Conrad, *An Outcast*, 162.

70 Ibid., 218.

3 Seeing Jim's Virtues in *Lord Jim: A Tale*

1 Joseph Conrad, *Lord Jim: A Tale* (Cambridge: Cambridge University Press, 2012), 172.

2 Ibid., 212.

3 *Lord Jim* was serialized in *Blackwood's Magazine* in 1899 and published by William Blackwood & Sons in 1900.

4 Aristotle, *Nicomachean Ethics, Aristotle's* Nicomachean Ethics, trans. Robert C. Bartlett and Susan D. Collins (Chicago: University of Chicago Press, 2011). The formulation implies not only sameness but also dialogue and self-knowledge. See Mavis Biss, "Aristotle on Friendship and Self-Knowledge: The Friend Beyond the Mirror," *History of Philosophy Quarterly* 28, no. 2 (April 2011): 125–40.

5 Conrad, "Author's Note" (1917), *Youth, Heart of Darkness, The End of the Tether*, ed. Owen Knowles (Cambridge: Cambridge University Press, 2012), 6.

6 Conrad, *Lord Jim*, 27.

7 Rumours are detached from an origin or author: Jim's flight from their unruly, ambiguously unsettling relation to the truth might be read as part of the modern condition that he wishes to escape. Jim's desire to escape his social world and circumstances anticipates Levinas's examination of the felt need to escape as the struggle with being itself: "Escape puts in question […] this alleged peace-with-self, since it aspires to break the chains of the I to the self." *On Escape/De l'évasion*, trans. Bettina Bergo (Stanford: Stanford University Press, 2003), 55.

8 Richard Ambrosini argues that Marlow is comparable to the Chorus in Greek tragedy – a reflection of Conrad's "search for a literary form more suited than adventure to give representation to the contradictions in the imperial project emerging by the late 1890s." "The Tragic Adventures: Conrad's and Marlow's Conflicting Narratives in *Lord Jim*," *The Conradian: The Journal of the Joseph Conrad Society (UK)* 38, no. 1 (Spring 2013): 53.

9 Paul Kintzele, "*Lord Jim*: Conrad's Fable of Judgment," *Journal of Modern Literature* 25, no. 2 (Winter 2000/2001): 71.

10 In John Lester's *Conrad and Religion* (London: The MacMillan Press, Ltd. 1988) we read that Jim is a "romantic egoist," but that his difference from the insidious Gentleman Brown, the man whose arrival in Patusan brings about Jim's tragic error in judgement, underlines the fact that he "is not totally self-seeking" (99). Lee Horsley similarly calls Jim "a romantic egoist" while acknowledging that Patusan is "not, as is sometimes argued [...] an untarnished, idyllic world," and that "Jim's storybook heroism has shown itself able to transform life in a temporary realization of the chivalric virtues of nobility, fidelity, and bravery." *Fictions of Power in English Literature: 1900–1950* (London: Routledge, 1995), 40–1. The chivalric virtues are theological interpretations of the classical tradition.

11 Garmon, Gerald M. *"Lord Jim* as Tragedy," *Conradiana: A Journal of Joseph Conrad Studies* 4, no. 1 (1972): 37.

12 See J.G. Finlayson's analysis of "Hegel's debt to Aristotle" in "Conflict and Reconciliation in Hegel's Theory of the Tragic," *Journal of the History of Philosophy* 37, no. 3 (July 1999): 493–520.

13 See chapter 2 note 7 of the present book.

14 A.C. Bradley, "Hegel's Theory of Tragedy," *Oxford Lectures on Poetry* (London: Macmillan and Co., 1909), 71.

15 Aristotle, *Poetics* 49b25–6.

16 For example, consider Fortinbras's arrival at the end of Shakespeare's *Hamlet*.

17 See Carnes Lord's persuasive interpretation of catharsis as the education, rather than the mere purgation or cleansing of emotion. *Education and Culture in the Political Thought of Aristotle* (Ithaca: Cornell University Press, 1982).

18 Richard Ambrosini argues that Conrad's contrast between the *Patna* crisis and Patusan itself embodies tragic conflict with roots in Aeschylus's *Oresteia*; Sophocles's *Antigone*; and *Hamlet*. "Tragic Adventures: Conrad's and Marlow's Conflicting Narratives in *Lord Jim*." *The Conradian: The Journal of the Joseph Conrad Society (UK)* 38, no. 1 (Spring 2013): 55.

19 Conrad, *Lord Jim*, 16.

20 Ibid., 11.

21 Ibid.

22 Ibid.

23 Ibid., 12.

24 Ibid.

25 Ibid., 13.

26 Ibid.

27 Ibid.

28 Robert Hampson argues that Willems and Jim are similar: "Jim is immobilized by real danger [during the crisis on the training ship],

but then, like Willems, preserves his self-ideal through a series of self-deceiving manoeuvres." *Joseph Conrad: Betrayal and Identity* (London: St. Martin's Press, 1992), 119. I suggest that the repetition throughout Conrad's *oeuvre* invites us to think through and recognize fine, but significant, distinctions between actions and between characters in a way that complicates claims about Jim's "self-deceiving manoeuvres" in contrast with Willems's self-deluded grandiosity. See chapter 1 of the present book.

29 Aristotle, *Nicomachean Ethics* 1115a24–b7.
30 Conrad, *Lord Jim*, 12.
31 Ibid., 118.
32 Ibid., 14.
33 Ibid., 14.
34 Ibid., 15.
35 Ibid.
36 Ibid.
37 Garmon rightly notes Conrad's "confident control of his design." "*Lord Jim* as Tragedy," 37.
38 Conrad, *Lord Jim*, 15.
39 Ibid., 16.
40 Ibid.
41 Ibid.
42 Ibid., 19.
43 Ibid., 21.
44 Ibid.
45 Aristotle, *Poetics*, 53b14–20.
46 Conrad, *Lord Jim*, 20.
47 Ibid., 27.
48 Ibid., 29.
49 Ibid., 28.
50 Ibid., 69.
51 Ibid., 108.
52 Ibid., 82.
53 Ibid., 84.
54 Garmon's argument that Jim embodies a realistic rendering of the tragic figure (unlike what Garmon claims is an unrealistic ancient standard of heroism) is persuasive to a point. Jim is humanized by his failure – and Aristotle's *Poetics* positions the tragic figure as admirable yet someone in whom an audience can recognize their own human possibilities. Conrad is clearly pointing out the absurdity of the modern condition (as fleshed out in the *Patna* crisis) in contrast to the comparable clarity of an ancient sphere of action (in the premodern society of Patusan). As ever, Conrad's

approach denies us a clear attribution of realism and fantasy to each setting: in many ways Patusan seems very "realistic" in contrast to the uncanny atmosphere aboard the modern steamer. See Garmon, *"Lord Jim as Tragedy,"* 34–40.

55 Conrad, *Lord Jim*, 81.
56 Ibid., 84.
57 Ibid., 95.
58 Ibid., 83.
59 Ibid., 79.
60 Ibid., 107.
61 Ibid., 109. Ellipses in original.
62 Ibid., 188.
63 The juxtaposition of achieved excellence with the illusion of/retrospective desire for primordial unity implicitly contrasts ancient metaphysics with modern critiques of metaphysical presence. The contrast anticipates Derrida but also Jacques Lacan's famous "Mirror Stage as Formative of the *I* Function as Revealed in Psychoanalytical Experience," *Écrits: The First Complete Edition in English,* trans. Bruce Fink (New York: W.W. Norton & Company), 75–81.
64 Conrad, *Lord Jim*, 185.
65 Ibid., 203.
66 Ibid., 173.
67 Ibid., 194.
68 Ibid.
69 Michael Valdez Moses shows how Conrad's portrayal of political conflict in Patusan is realistic, based on historical fact. See "Conrad, The Flight from Modernity," *The Novel and the Globalization of Culture* (New York: Oxford University Press, 1995), 77.
70 Lord Jim is, for example, both "master" and "captive." Conrad, *Lord Jim*, 188.
71 Conrad, *Lord Jim*, 215.
72 Ibid., 218.
73 Ibid., 209.
74 Ibid., 188.
75 Moses, "Conrad, The Flight from Modernity," 72.
76 Conrad, *Lord Jim*, 198.
77 Ibid., 188.
78 Ibid., 213.
79 Ibid., 313.
80 Ibid., 264.
81 Ibid., 265.
82 Ibid., 286.

83　Ibid., 292.

84　Ibid., 101.

85　Ibid., 230.

86　Ibid., 291.

87　Ibid., 303.

88　Ibid., 307.

89　Aristotle, *Poetics* 49b25–6.

90　Conrad, *Lord Jim*, 312.

91　Ibid., 107.

92　Ibid., 48.

93　Ibid., 65.

94　Ibid., 48.

95　This audience implicitly includes the reader. As Laurence Davies argues, the pursuit of the truth in *Lord Jim* is not autodidactic but shared, tied to dialogue and bound up with community. See "'The Thing Which Was Not' and The Thing That Is Also: Conrad's Ironic Foreshadowing," *Conrad in the Twenty-First Century: Contemporary Approaches and Perspectives*, eds. Carola Kaplan et. al. (New York: Routledge, 2005), 233.

96　Zdzisław Najder "*Lord Jim*: A Romantic Tragedy of Honour," *Conrad in Perspective: Essays on Art and Fidelity* (Cambridge: Cambridge University Press, 2005), 82.

97　See James Phelan's especially clear description of the character narrator's role in "*Lord Jim* and the Uses of Textual Recalcitrance," *Joseph Conrad: Voice, Sequence, History, Genre*, eds. Jakob Lothe, Jeremy Hawthorn, and James Phelan (Columbus: The Ohio State University, 2008), 44–5.

98　Conrad, *Lord Jim*, 123.

99　Phelan, "Lord Jim and the Uses of Textual Recalcitrance," 56.

100　Conrad, *Lord Jim*, 122.

101　Ibid.

102　Ibid., 75. Ellipses in original.

103　Ibid., 39.

104　Conrad's "mystery" here and throughout his *oeuvre* may affirm metaphysical presence (Jim's true self beneath mere appearances); and yet it may also anticipate Heidegger's "mystery" of being, his effort to uncover the question of being precluded by the presence/absence binary in the history of metaphysics.

105　Conrad, *Lord Jim*, 101.

106　Such a position anticipates Jacques Derrida's ethics of undecidability.

107　Conrad, *Lord Jim*, 75.

108　Ibid.

109 To William Blackwood, 31 May 1902, *Collected Letters, Volume 2, 1898–1902*, eds. Frederick R. Karl and Laurence Davies (Cambridge: Cambridge University Press, 1986), 418.

110 Conrad, *Lord Jim*, 90.

111 Ibid., 75.

112 Ibid., 135.

113 Ibid., 50.

114 Ibid., 124.

115 As Zdzisław Najder eloquently puts it, in discussing Jim's ultimate sacrifice, "having lifted his hero onto the tragic pedestal, Conrad shuns any simple-minded illusions." "*Lord Jim, A Romantic Tragedy of Honour*," *Conrad in Perspective: Essays on Art and Fidelity* (Cambridge: Cambridge University Press, 1997), 93.

116 Conrad, *Lord Jim*, 171.

117 Ibid., 33.

118 Ibid., 16.

119 Conrad, *Heart of Darkness, Youth, Heart of Darkness, The End of the Tether*, ed. Owen Knowles (Cambridge: Cambridge University Press, 2012), 93.

120 Conrad, *Lord Jim*, 257–8.

121 Ibid., 166.

122 Ibid., 134.

4 The Discerning Narrator in *Falk: A Reminiscence*

1 Joseph Conrad, *Falk: A Reminiscence*, Typhoon and Other Tales (Oxford: Oxford World's Classics, 2002), 120.

2 Ibid.

3 Joel R. Kehler, "The Centrality of the Narrator in Conrad's 'Falk,'" *Conradiana: A Journal of Joseph Conrad Studies* 6.1 (1974): 28.

4 Tony Tanner, "'Gnawed Bones' and 'Artless Tales:' Eating and Narrative in Falk," *Joseph Conrad: A Commemoration*, ed. Norman Sherry (London: MacMillan, 1976), 21.

5 Falk reflects a wide range of modern philosophical ideas linked to modern primitivism found in Rousseau, Darwin, and Schopenhauer.

6 Conrad, *Falk*, 120.

7 Ibid.

8 Ibid.

9 Ibid., 82; 76.

10 Ibid., 129.

11 Ibid.

12 Ibid., 85.

13 Ibid., 83.
14 Ibid., 85.
15 Tanner, "Eating and Narrative," 21.
16 Conrad, *Falk*, 84.
17 Ibid., 80; 83.
18 Ibid., 79; 83.
19 Ibid., 79.
20 Ibid.
21 Ibid., 80.
22 Nietzsche, *Thus Spake Zarathustra: A Book for Everyone and Nobody*, trans. Graham Parkes (Oxford: Oxford University Press, 2008), 16.
23 Daphna Erdinast-Vulcan, *The Strange Short Fiction of Writing, Culture, and Subjectivity* (Oxford: Oxford University Press, 1999), 97.
24 Conrad, *Falk*, 79–80.
25 Ibid., 122.
26 Ibid., 132.
27 Harry Sewlall, "Cannibalism in the Colonial Imaginary: A Reading of Joseph Conrad's 'Falk,'" *JLS/TLW* (June 2006): 165.
28 Nietzsche, "On Ethics," *The Portable Nietzsche*, ed. & trans. Walter Kaufman (London: Viking Penguin, 1982), 31.
29 Paul Vlitos, "Conrad's Ideas of Gastronomy: Dining in 'Falk,'" *Victorian Literature and Culture* 36 (2008): 438.
30 Tanner, "Eating and Narrative," 21.
31 Conrad, *Falk*, 85.
32 Ibid., 143.
33 The conversation recalls *An Outcast*'s Lingard who deepens his thinking about justice when he hears himself speak the word ("justice"). Both instances register a modern awareness of language as language, but they may also be read as affirmations of Socratic dialogue.
34 Conrad, *Falk*, 85.
35 Ibid., 91.
36 Ibid., 118.
37 Ibid., 121.
38 Ibid., 100.
39 Ibid., 89.
40 Ibid.
41 Ibid., 109.
42 Ibid., 115.
43 Ibid., 116.
44 Aristotle, *Politics* 1.i., 1253a, trans. T.A. Sinclair and Trevor J. Saunders (London: Penguin, 1992).
45 Conrad, *Falk*, 130.

46 Ibid., 127.

47 Aristotle, Book 8, *Aristotle's Nicomachean Ethics: A New Translation*, trans. Robert C. Bartlett and Susan D. Collins (Chicago: University of Chicago Press, 2011).

48 Critics debate how to read this opening line. My reading is straightforward, keeping in mind Aristotle's naturalistic political theory. Basing her definition of politics on Aristotle, philosopher Agnes Callard explains that we share sociality with animals, but not our political nature (which is bound up with *logos* – reason and speech): "To say that we're political means that we live together under a shared idea of how to do so." "Socratic Politics," 2021 Nuveen Lecture with Agnes Callard, University of Chicago Divinity School, YouTube video, 1:14:58, 12 October 2021, https://www.youtube.com/watch?v=AwFI_t3YHPs.

49 For Aristotle this idea is linked to procreation in his naturalistic politics. In *Chance* Marlow reflects that "of all the forms offered to us by life it is the one demanding a couple to realize it fully, which is the most imperative. Pairing off is the fate of mankind." Conrad, *Chance: A Tale in Two Parts* (Oxford: Oxford University Press, 1988), 426.

50 Conrad, *Falk,* 115.

51 Ibid., 121.

52 Kehler, "The Centrality of the Narrator," 26.

53 Conrad, *Falk,* 120.

54 Aristotle, *Nicomachean Ethics* 1143a.

55 The term "doxa" is not straightforward throughout Aristotle's *oeuvre*. I rely on Aristotle's use of the term to distinguish between a lower kind of knowledge such as opinions or received ideas and higher knowledge of universals.

56 Conrad, *Falk,* 135.

57 Nussbaum, "Equity and Mercy," *Sex and Social Justice* (Oxford: Oxford University Press, 1999), 159.

58 Ibid., 161.

59 For a careful analysis of the difference between forgiveness and *suggnōmē* in Aristotle's ethics, see Clarissa Phillips-Garret, "*Sungnōmē* in Aristotle," *Apeiron* 50 no. 3 (2017): 311–33.

60 Walter E. Anderson, "'Falk': Conrad's Tale of Evolution.' *Studies in Short Fiction* 25, no. 2 (Spring, 1988): 106.

61 Rosalind Hursthouse draws attention to Aristotle's concern not only with passions before or during an act but also feelings after actions as reflections of character. "Acting and Feeling in Character: *Nicomachean Ethics* 3.i," *Phronesis* (May 1984): 252–66.

62 Phillips-Garret, 320–1.

63 Conrad, *Falk,* 100.

64 Owen Knowles and Gene Moore note that Conrad's source may have
been a story of cannibalism at sea reported in the *Times* (7 November
1884), whereby the two men were originally sentenced to death but were
eventually sentenced to six months in jail based on the circumstances of
their actions. See the *Oxford Reader's Companion to Conrad* (London: Oxford
University Press, 2000), 124.

65 Conrad, *Falk*, 135.

66 Ibid.

67 In *Poetics* 61a31–b5, trans. Richard Janko (Cambridge: Hackett, 1987)
Aristotle discusses critics who base their judgements on "some prior
assumption, and judging it right themselves make inferences [from it]."

68 Conrad, *Falk*, 134.

69 *Falk*'s implicitly sceptical outlook on consistent or coherent, pre-linguistic
origins and self-sufficiency anticipates Jacques Derrida, especially *Of
Grammatology* (1974), trans. Gayatri Chakravorty Spivak (Baltimore: Johns
Hopkins University Press, 2016).

70 Aristotle writes, "…not every sound made by an animal is voice, for it
is possible to make a sound also with the tongue or as in coughing); but
that which does the striking must have a soul and there must be a certain
imagination." Book II *De Anima [On the soul]*, trans. J.A. Smith, *The Basic
Works of Aristotle*, ed. R. McKeon (New York: Random House, 1971).

71 Interestingly, Falk might embody the origin of language (Rousseau) and,
in discovering his inability to live alone, the origin of politics (Aristotle).

72 Conrad, *Falk*, 77.

73 Ibid., 132.

74 Ibid., 144.

75 Ibid.

76 Ibid., 137.

77 Ibid., 139.

78 Aristotle, *Nicomachean Ethics* 1115b7.

79 Conrad, *Heart of Darkness*, Youth, Heart of Darkness, The End of the Tether
(Cambridge: Cambridge University Press, 2010), 103.

80 Conrad, *Falk*, 137.

81 Ibid., 138.

82 Ibid., 139.

83 Aristotle, *Nicomachean Ethics* 1115b11–14.

84 Conrad, *Falk*, 139.

85 Ibid., 116.

86 Conrad, *Falk*, 79. "Mystery" is a Conradian term dense with meaning.
Here he seems to want to preserve a sense of philosophical wonder
for "the unchanging sea." The adjective "unchanging" does not mean
that the object it describes can be fully known or totalized but that it is

possibly knowable – as in something to be known or discovered. This idea might appeal to Derrida's ethics to come/à venir. Conrad's sea is, after all, a literally fluid, unstable "ground" that is always permeated or "contaminated" by chance and the unpredictable, and therefore opens onto possible, always incomplete knowledge.

87 Ibid., 82.

5. Marlow's Practical Wisdom: *Chance: A Tale in Two Parts*

1 Conrad, *Chance: A Tale in Two Parts* (Oxford: Oxford World's Classics, 1988), 446.

2 Ibid., 272.

3 Ibid., 137.

4 For example, Max Hermens focuses on the intentional thematic and narratological continuities between *Chance*, *Lord Jim*, *Heart of Darkness*, and "Youth": "*Chance* actually alludes to Marlow's other appearances and continues previously established discussions on authorship." See "More than a Voice from the Darkness: Charlie Marlow and the Posture of an Invented Author," *Neophilologus* 101, no. 1 (Jan. 2017): 170.

5 John G. Peters, "'Let that Marlow talk': *Chance* and the Narrative Problem of Marlow," *The Conradian: The Journal of the Joseph Conrad Society (UK)* 39.1 (Spring 2014): 133.

6 Ibid., 144. This argument implicitly takes up Bruce Harkness's claim that in the novel, "chance does not [wholly] govern life." See Bruce Harkness, "The Epigraph of Conrad's 'Chance,'" *Nineteenth-Century Fiction* 9, no. 3 (1954): 211.

7 Conrad, *Chance*, 3.

8 Ibid., 4.

9 Aristotle, *Nicomachean Ethics* 1140a, *Aristotle's Nicomachean Ethics: A New Translation*, trans. Robert C. Bartlett and Susan D. Collins (Chicago: University of Chicago Press, 2011).

10 Aristotle, *The Metaphysics* 982b, Book Alpha, trans. Hugh Lawson-Tancred (London: Penguin, 2004).

11 Conrad, *Chance*, 272.

12 Aristotle, *Ethics*, 1140a; 1140b5–7.

13 Ibid., 1106b36.

14 Ibid., 1106b21–3.

15 Martha Nussbaum describes practical wisdom as "the interplay of universal rule and particular perception." *The Fragility of Goodness: Luck and Ethics in Greek Tragedy and Philosophy* (Cambridge University Press, 1986), 291. Howard Cuzer points out the complexity of the doctrine of the mean which is too often misunderstood as a Goldilocks-type theory: "Indeed, how to utilize the doctrine of the mean is not obvious." *Aristotle and the Virtues* (Oxford: Oxford University Press, 2012), 51.

16 Aristotle, Book Alpha, *Metaphysics* 981a.
17 Stephen Salkever, *Finding the Mean: Theory and Practice in Aristotelian Political Philosophy* (Princeton: Princeton University Press, 1990), 72–3. Thomas Pfau defines *phronēsis* as "at once generative of and continually tested and revised by its dialectical 'process of transmission.'" *Minding the Modern: Human Agency, Intellectual Traditions, and Responsible Knowledge* (Indiana: University of Notre Dame 2013), 56.
18 Aristide Tessitore explains that Aristotle distinguishes between virtuous actions and an authentically virtuous character: "[W]hile it is neither necessary nor possible to possess virtue in order to become virtuous, one can and must cultivate the external actions appropriate to virtue as a part of the process of becoming genuinely virtuous." *Reading Aristotle's Ethics* (New York: SUNY Press, 1996), 26.
19 Aristotle, *Nicomachean Ethics* 1142b10–15.
20 Conrad, *Chance*, 22; 23.
21 Marlow's conversation with Powell also reflects what Debra Romanick Baldwin compares to a classical "fostering [of] dialectical difficult, puzzlement and curiosity." See "Marlow, Socrates and an Ancient Quarrel in *Chance*," *Centennial Essays on Conrad's* Chance, Alan H. Simmons and Susan Jones, eds. (Leiden: Brill, 2016), 53–65.
22 See "Marlow's Morality," *Philosophy and Literature* 27, no. 2 (October 2003): 318. Brudney's main ally here is Iris Murdoch. He writes, "let's take attentiveness to the other as the virtue corresponding to the vice of narcissism" (325).
23 Conrad, *Chance*, 23.
24 Conrad, "Author's Note" (1920), *Chance* (Oxford: Oxford World's Classics, 1988), xxxiv.
25 Conrad, *Chance*, 23.
26 Ibid., 24.
27 Ibid.
28 Steven Wall, "Perfectionism in Moral and Political Philosophy," *The Stanford Encyclopedia of Philosophy* (Fall 2008 Edition), Edward N. Zalta ed. http://plato.stanford.edu/archives/fall2008/entries/perfectionism-moral/.
29 Aristotle, *Nicomachean Ethics* 1104b5–13.
30 Conrad, *Chance*, 57.
31 Ibid., 188.
32 Ibid., 59.
33 Ford Madox Ford, "Mr. John Galsworthy," Literary Portraits from *The Tribune* (1907), *Ford Madox Ford: Critical Essays* (Manchester: Carcanet Press Ltd., 2002), 34.
34 Conrad, *Chance*, 39; 42.
35 Ibid., 45.

36 Ibid., 134.

37 Ibid., 134–5.

38 Julia Annas, "Which Variety of Virtue Ethics?," *Varieties of Virtue Ethics*, eds. David Carr, James Arthur, and Kristján Kristjánsson (London: Palgrave Macmillan, 2017), 37.

39 Conrad, *Chance*, 37; 310.

40 Ibid., 292.

41 Martin Ray, Introduction, *Chance: A Tale in Two Parts* (Oxford: Oxford University Press, 1988), xviii. Gail Fraser makes a similar point in "Mediating between the Sexes: Conrad's *Chance*," *The Review of English Studies* 43, no. 169 (Feb. 1992), 81–8. Fraser challenges feminist critiques of the novel by showing how Marlow's view is balanced yet nuanced as he "mediates between two different [stereotypically masculine and feminine] views of the world" (81).

42 Aristotle, *Nicomachean Ethics* 1142b1–6.

43 Flora's position along a precipice potentially groups her with other threshold characters – including those that transgress or "overstep" – throughout Conrad's *oeuvre*. In any case as Marlow and Mrs. Fyne's fears suggest, Flora is a destabilizing figure in the novel: literally, with one misstep she might die; figuratively with one misstep she might become a "fallen" woman.

44 Conrad, *Chance*, 58.

45 Ibid., 59.

46 Ibid.

47 Ibid.

48 Salkever cites the *Nicomahcean Ethics* Book 6, 1144a6–9, in *Finding*, 76.

49 See Winne Verloc in *The Secret Agent*: she is admirable yet pathetic, not tragic. Conrad, *The Secret Agent: A Simple Tale* (Cambridge: Cambridge University Press, 2013).

50 In *Fragility*, Nussbaum cites Aristotle's architecture metaphor in support of his original notion of a flexible ethics: "Aristotle tells us that a person who attempts to make every decision by appealing to some antecedent general principle held firm and inflexible for the occasion is like an architect who tries to use a straight ruler on the intricate curves of a fluted column" (301). A similar Aristotelian claim that theory is useless when dissociated from practice can be found in Jane Austen. See David Gallop, "Jane Austen and the Aristotelian Ethic," *Philosophy and Literature* 23, no. 1 (1999): 96–109.

51 Conrad, *Chance*, 193.

52 Ibid., 187–8.

53 Ibid., 190.

54 Gallop translates *Nicomachean Ethics* 1105b13–15 as follows: "Most people [...] by taking refuge in arguments (*logoi*), think that they are engaged in

philosophy, and that they will become good in that way. "Jane Austen and the Aristotelian Ethic," 99.

55 Salkever *Finding*, 64–5.

56 Conrad, *Chance*, 126.

57 Ibid., 38.

58 Ibid., 51.

59 Ibid., 38–9.

60 Ibid., 38.

61 Conrad's implicit critique of Zoë Fyne's theory anticipates what Giorgio Agamben calls biopower (following Foucault's biopolitics) – where politics exploits or exerts power over humanity by reducing "life" to bare life – mere bodies that can be controlled and destroyed. *Homo Sacer: Sovereign Power and Bare Life*, trans. Daniel Heller-Roazen (Stanford: Stanford University Press), 1998. Agamben argues that biopower is possible because we have lost Aristotle's distinction between *zoë* (bare life) and *bios* (ways of life). J.G. Finlayson, however, points out that Aristotle uses *zoë* to mean "life, or living, or (just like bios) way of living [...] in a wide nonpejorative sense." "Bare Life" and Politics in Agamben's Reading of Aristotle," *The Review of Politics* 72 (2010): 108.

62 Conrad, *Chance*, 194.

63 Ibid., 191.

64 To Edward Garnett, 15 March 1895, *The Collected Letters of Joseph Conrad, Volume 1: 1857–1897*, eds. Fredric Karl and Laurence Davies (Cambridge: Cambridge University Press, 1983).

65 To Edward Garnett, 20 July 1905, *The Collected Letters of Joseph Conrad, Volume 3: 1903–1907*, eds. Fredric Karl and Laurence Davies (Cambridge: Cambridge University Press, 1988).

66 Conrad, *Victory: An Island Tale* (Cambridge: Cambridge University Press, 2016), 73.

67 Conrad, *Chance*, 187.

68 Ibid., 49.

69 Ibid., 25.

70 Ibid., 279.

71 Ibid., 329.

72 Ibid., 263. Emphasis in original.

73 Ibid., 331.

74 Marlow's claim that Flora's familiarity with Anthony's face interferes with their relationship approaches Emmanuel Levinas's ethics of the other, *l'autrui*. For Levinas, interpreting the face erases the other and precludes any possibility of an ethical relation. The face invites one to encounter the undeniable reality of the other, for "the face speaks to me and thereby invites me to a relation." *Totality and Infinity: An Essay on*

Exteriority, trans. Alphonso Lingis (Pittsburg: Duquesne University Press, 1969), 198.

75 Conrad, *Chance*, 272.

76 Annas, "Which Variety of Virtue Ethics?," 37.

77 Conrad, *Chance*, 282.

78 Ibid., 276–7.

79 Ibid., 293–4.

80 Ibid., 401.

81 Ibid., 411–12.

82 Ibid., 424.

83 Ibid., 413.

84 Ibid., 416.

85 Roger Crisp writes that practical wisdom "is closely related to common sense, except that its sphere is that of the virtues as a whole" and is not simply about perceptiveness and judgement but also action, the capacity to give oneself orders. Introduction, *Aristotle, Nicomachean Ethics* (Cambridge: Cambridge University Press, 1999), xxv.

86 Conrad, *Chance*, 145.

87 Ibid., 282.

88 This passage comes from GENN Manuscript 1207, Beinecke Rare Book and Manuscript Library, Yale University, page 289. Debra Romanick Baldwin kindly sent me pictures of pages 288–90 from her visit to the library in 2015.

Conclusion: "Speakings"

1 "… reports of ships met and signalled at sea, name, port, where from, where bound for so many days out, ending frequently with the words 'All well.'" Conrad, *The Mirror of the Sea* (Oxford: Oxford World's Classics, 1988), 57.

2 Conrad, "Author's Note" (1920), *Chance: A Tale in Two Parts* (Oxford: Oxford World's Classics, 1988), xxxiii–xxxiv.

3 Aristotle, *Poetics* 49b25–9, trans. Richard Janko (Indianapolis: Hackett, 1987).

4 To William Blackwood, 31 May 1902, *Collected Letters of Joseph Conrad, Volume 2: 1898–1902*, eds. Frederick R. Karl and Laurence Davies (Cambridge: Cambridge University Press, 1986), 418.

5 Conrad, *Falk: A Reminiscence*, Typhoon and Other Tales (Oxford: Oxford World's Classics, 2002), 120.

6 To Richard Curle, 17 July 1923, qtd. in Eloise Knapp Hay, *The Political Novels of Joseph Conrad: A Critical with a New Preface* (Chicago: University of Chicago Press, 1981), 5.

7 Conrad, *Chance*, 276–7.

Bibliography

Acharaïou, Amar. *Rethinking Post-colonialism: Colonialist Discourse in Modern Literature and the Legacy of Classical Writers*. London: Palgrave Macmillan, 2008.

Adams, David. *Colonial Odysseys: Empire and Epic in the Modernist Novel*. Ithaca: Cornell University Press, 2003.

Agamben, Giorgio. *Homo Sacer: Sovereign Power and Bare Life*. Translated by Daniel Heller-Roazen. Palo Alto, CA: Stanford University Press, 1998.

Agathon. Quoted in *Aristotle's* Nicomachean Ethics*: A New Translation*, 1140a20. Translated by Robert C. Bartlett and Susan Collins. Chicago: Chicago University Press, 2012.

Ambrosini, Richard. "Tragic Adventures: Conrad's and Marlow's Conflicting Narratives in *Lord Jim*." *The Conradian: Journal of the Joseph Conrad Society (UK)* 38, no. 1 (Spring 2013): 53–71.

Anderson, Walter E. "'Falk:' Conrad's Tale of Evolution." *Studies in Short Fiction* 25, no. 2 (Spring 1988): 101–8.

Annas, Julia. "Which Variety of Virtue Ethics?" In *Varieties of Virtue Ethics*, edited by David Carr, James Arthur, and Kristján Kristjánsson, 35–51. London: Palgrave Macmillan, 2017.

Aristotle. *The Art of Rhetoric*. Translated by H.C. Lawson-Tancred. Oxford: Oxford University Press, 1991.

– *De Anima (On the Soul)*. Translated by J.A. Smith. In *The Basic Works of Aristotle*, edited by R. McKeon, 533–603. New York: Random House, 1971.

– *The Metaphysics*. Translated by H.C. Lawson-Tancred. London: Penguin, 2004.

– *Nicomachean Ethics: A New Translation*. Translated by Robert C. Bartlett and Susan D. Collins. Chicago: University of Chicago Press, 2011.

– *Physics*. Translated by Robin Waterfield. Oxford: Oxford World's Classics, 1996.

– *Poetics*. Translated by Richard Janko. Indianapolis: Hackett, 1987.

– *The Politics*. Translated by T.A. Sinclair. London: Penguin, 1962.

Artese, Brian. *Testimony on Trial: Conrad, James, and the Contest for Modernism*. Toronto: University of Toronto Press, 2012.

Attridge, Derrick. *The Singularity of Literature*. London: Routledge, 2004.

Baldwin, Debra Romanick. "Marlow, Socrates, and an Ancient Quarrel in *Chance*." In *Centennial Essays on Conrad's* Chance, edited by Alan H. Simmons and Susan Jones, 53–65. Leiden: Brill, 2016.

– "Conrad's *Victory* and *The Shadow-Line*." In *A Joseph Conrad Companion*, edited by Leonard Orr and Ted Billy, 231–52. Westport, CT: Greenwood Press, 1999.

– "'The Worker in Prose': Conrad's Anti-Theoretical Theory of Art." In *Conrad's Century: The Past and Future Splendour*, edited by Laura L. Davis, 189–202. New York: Columbia University Press, 1998.

Baxter, Katherine Isobel. "Comedy and Romance: A New Look at Conrad and Shakespeare." In *Joseph Conrad and the Performing Arts*, edited by Katherine Isobel Baxter and Sean Hand, 111–26. Surrey: Ashgate, 2009.

– *Joseph Conrad and the Swan Song of Romance*. Surrey: Ashgate, 2010.

Behler, Ernst. *German Romantic Literary Theory*. Cambridge: Cambridge University Press, 1993.

Biss, Mavis. "Aristotle on Friendship and Self-Knowledge: The Friend Beyond the Mirror." *History of Philosophy Quarterly* 28, no. 2 (April 2011): 125–40.

Bowen, Elizabeth. *The Collected Stories*. New York: Vintage, 1981.

Bowers, Terence. "Conrad's *Aeneid*: *Heart of Darkness* and the Classical Epic." *Conradiana: A Journal of Joseph Conrad Studies*. 38, no. 2 (Summer 2006): 115–42.

Bradley, A.C. "Hegel's Theory of Tragedy." In *Oxford Lectures on Poetry*, 69–95. London: Macmillan and Co., 1909.

Brudney, Daniel. "Marlow's Morality." *Philosophy and Literature* 27, no. 2 (October 2003): 318–40.

Callard, Agnes. "Socratic Politics." 2021 Nuveen Lecture with Agnes Callard. University of Chicago Divinity School. Youtube video, 1:14:58. 12 October 2021. https://www.youtube.com/watch?v=AwFI_t3YHPs.

Caputo, John D. *The Prayers and Tears of Jacques Derrida*. Bloomington, IN: Indiana University Press, 1997.

Carlson, Matthew Paul. "Conrad's Early Fiction and the Aesthetic of Dehumanization." *The Conradian: The Journal of the Joseph Conrad Society (UK)* 36, no. 1 (2011): 14–29.

Clark, Lorraine. "Rousseau and Political Compassion in *The N[*****] of the 'Narcissus.'*"*Conradiana: A Journal of Joseph Conrad Studies* 31, no. 2 (1999): 120–30.

Conrad, Joseph. *Chance: A Tale in Two Parts*. Edited by Martin Ray. Oxford: Oxford World's Classics, 1988.

– *The Collected Letters, Vol. 1: 1861–1897*. Edited by Fredrick R. Karl and Laurence Davies. Cambridge: Cambridge University Press, 1983.
– *The Collected Letters of Joseph Conrad, Volume 2: 1898–1902*. Edited by Frederick R. Karl and Laurence Davies. Cambridge: Cambridge University Press, 1986.
– *The Collected Letters of Joseph Conrad, Volume 3: 1903–1907*. Edited by Fredric Karl and Laurence Davies. Cambridge: Cambridge University Press, 1988.
– *Falk: A Reminiscence*. In *Typhoon and Other Tales*, edited by Cedric Watts, 77–145. Oxford: Oxford World's Classics, 2002.
– *Heart of Darkness*. Edited by Owen Knowles and Allan H. Simmons. Cambridge: Cambridge University Press, 2018.
– *Lord Jim: A Tale*. Edited by J.H. Stape and Ernest W. Sullivan II. Cambridge: Cambridge University Press, 2012.
– *The Mirror of the Sea*. In *The Mirror of the Sea* and *A Personal Record*, edited by Zdzisław Najder, 3–194. Oxford: Oxford World's Classics, 1988.
– *An Outcast of the Islands*. Edited by Alan H. Simmons. Cambridge: Cambridge University Press, 2016.
– *A Personal Record*. Edited by Zdzisław Najder and J.H. Stape. Cambridge: Cambridge University Press, 2008.
– Preface. In *The N[*****] of the "Narcissus," Typhoon, The Shadow-Line*, 3–6. London: J.M. Dent & Sons Ltd., 1945.
– *The Secret Agent: A Simple Tale*. Edited by Jacques Berthoud and J.H. Stape. Cambridge: Cambridge University Press, 2013.
– *The Shadow-Line, A Confession*. Edited by J.H. Stape and Allan H. Simmons with Owen Knowles. Cambridge: Cambridge University Press, 2013.
– *Victory: An Island Tale*. Edited by J.H. Stape and Alexandre Fachard. Cambridge: Cambridge University Press, 2016.
– *Youth, Heart of Darkness, The End of the Tether*. Edited by Owen Knowles. Cambridge: Cambridge University Press, 2010.
Coroneos, Con. *Space, Conrad, and Modernity*. Oxford: Oxford University Press, 2002.
Crisp, Roger. "Introduction." In Aristotle's *Nicomachean Ethics*, vii–xxxv. Translated by Roger Crisp. Cambridge: Cambridge University Press, 1999.
Curle, Richard. *The Last Twelve Years of Conrad*. Garden City, NY: Doubleday, Doran and Company, Inc., 1928.
Cuzer, Howard. *Aristotle and the Virtues*. Oxford: Oxford University Press, 2012.
Davies, Laurence. "'The Thing Which Was Not' and The Thing That Is Also: Conrad's Ironic Foreshadowing." In *Conrad in the Twenty-First Century: Contemporary Approaches and Perspectives*, edited by Carola Kaplan, Peter Lancelot Mallios, and Andrea White, 223–37. New York: Routledge, 2005.

Derrida, Jacques. *The Gift of Death*. Translated by David Wills. Chicago: University of Chicago Press, 1995.

– *Given Time 1: Counterfeit Money*. Translated by Peggy Kamuf. Chicago: University of Chicago Press, 1992.

– *Politics of Friendship*. Translated by George Collins. New York: Verso, 1997.

Drake, Ryan. "Wonder, Nature and the Ends of Tragedy." *International Philosophical Quarterly* 50, no. 107 (March 2010): 77–91.

Eagleton, Terry. *Sweet Violence: The Idea of the Tragic*. Oxford: Wiley-Blackwell, 2002.

– *Trouble with Strangers*. Oxford: Wiley-Blackwell, 2009.

Epstein, Hugh. "Conrad and Nature, 1900–1904." In *Conrad and Nature: Essays*, edited by Lissa Schneider-Rebozo, Jeffrey Mathes McCarthy, and John G. Peters, 173–95. London: Routledge, 2018.

Erdinast-Vulcan, Daphna. *Joseph Conrad and the Modern Temper*. Cambridge: Cambridge University Press, 1991.

– *The Strange Short Fiction of Joseph Conrad: Writing, Culture, and Subjectivity*. Cambridge: Cambridge University Press, 1999.

Faure, Murray. "Understanding Aristotle's Prudence and Its Resurgence in Postmodern Times." *Phronimon* 14, no. 2 (2013): 45–84.

Finlayson, James Gordon. "'Bare Life' and Politics in Agamben's Reading of Aristotle." *The Review of Politics* 72 (2010): 97–126.

– "Conflict and Reconciliation in Hegel's Theory of the Tragic." *Journal of the History of Philosophy* 37, no. 3 (July 1999): 493–520.

Fleishman, Avrom. *Conrad's Politics: Community and Anarchy in the Fiction of Joseph Conrad*. Baltimore: Johns Hopkins Press, 1967.

Ford, Madox Ford. "Mr. John Galsworthy." Literary Portraits from *The Tribune* (1907). In *Ford Madox Ford: Critical Essays*, edited by Max Saunders and Richard Stang, 33–6. Manchester: Carcanet Press Ltd., 2002.

Fraser, Gail. "Mediating between the Sexes: Conrad's *Chance*." *The Review of English Studies* 43, no. 169 (Feb. 1992): 81–8.

Gallop, David. "Jane Austen and the Aristotelian Ethic." *Philosophy and Literature* 23, no. 1 (1999): 96–109.

Gard, Roger, ed. *Henry James: The Critical Heritage*. London. Routledge, 1982.

Garmon, Gerald M. "*Lord Jim* as Tragedy." *Conradiana: A Journal of Joseph Conrad Studies* 41, no. 1 (1972): 34–40.

Graham, Kenneth. "Conrad and Modernism." *The Cambridge Companion to Joseph Conrad*, edited by J.H. Stape, 203–22. Cambridge: Cambridge University Press, 1996.

Greany, Michael. *Conrad, Language, and Narrative*. Cambridge: Cambridge University Press, 2002.

Griffith, John Wylie. *Conrad and the Anthropological Dilemma: "Bewildered traveler."* Oxford: Clarendon Press, 1995.

Halliwell, Stephen. "Commentary." *The* Poetics *of Aristotle*, 69–184. Chapel Hill: University of North Carolina Press, 1987.

– Epilogue: The *Poetics* and Its Interpreters. In *Essays on Aristotle's* Poetics, Edited by Amélie Rorty, 409–24. Princeton: Princeton University Press, 1992.

Hampson, Robert. *Joseph Conrad: Betrayal and Identity*. London: St. Martin's Press, 1992.

Harkness, Bruce. "The Epigraph of Conrad's 'Chance,'" *Nineteenth-Century Fiction* 9, no. 3 (1954): 209–22.

Harpham, Geoffrey Galt. *One of Us: The Mastery of Joseph Conrad*. Chicago: University of Chicago Press 1996.

Hawthorn, Jeremy. Explanatory Notes. In Joseph Conrad's *Under Western Eyes*, edited by Jeremy Hawthorn, 284–304. Oxford: Oxford University Press, 2003.

– "Life Sentences: Linearity and Its Discontents in *An Outcast of the Islands*." In *Joseph Conrad: Voice, Sequence, History, Genre*, edited by Jacob Lothe, Jeremy Hawthorn, and James Phelan, 83–99. Columbus: The Ohio State University Press, 2008.

Horsley, Lee. *Fictions of Power in English Literature: 1900–1950*. London: Routledge, 1995.

Hume, David. "Concerning Moral Sentiment." Appendix 1. In *An Enquiry Concerning the Principles of Morals*, edited by J.B. Schneewind, 82–8. Indianapolis: Hackett, 1983.

Huneker, James. "The Genius of Joseph Conrad." *The North American Review* 200, no. 705 (August 1914): 270–9.

Hursthouse, Rosalind. "Acting and Feeling in Character: *Nicomachean Ethics* 3.i." *Phronesis* (May 1984): 252–66.

Ingram, Alan, ed. *Joseph Conrad: Selected Literary Criticism and* The Shadow-Line. New York: Metheuen, 1986.

Kehler, Joel R. "The Centrality of the Narrator in Conrad's 'Falk.'" *Conradiana: A Journal of Joseph Conrad Studies* 6, no. 1 (1974): 19–30.

Kintzele, Paul. "*Lord Jim*: Conrad's Fable of Judgment." *Journal of Modern Literature* 25, no. 2 (Winter 2000/2001): 69–79.

Knapp Hay, Eloise. *The Political Novels of Joseph Conrad: A Critical Study with a New Preface*. Chicago: University of Chicago Press, 1981.

Knowles, Owen, and Gene M. Moore. *The Oxford Reader's Companion to Conrad*. London: Oxford University Press, 2000.

Lacan, Jacques. "Mirror Stage as Formative of the *I* Function as Revealed in Psychoanalytical Experience." In *Écrits: The First Complete Edition in English*. Translated by Bruce Fink, 75–81. New York: W.W. Norton & Company, 2006.

Lester, John. *Conrad and Religion*. London: Palgrave Macmillan, 1988.

Levinas, Emmanuel. *On Escape/De l'évasion*. Translated by Bettina Bergo. Stanford: Stanford University Press, 2003.

– *Totality and Infinity: An Essay on Exteriority*. Translated by Alphonso Lingis. Pittsburgh: Duquesne University Press, 1969.

Lord, Carnes. *Education and Culture in the Political Thought of Aristotle*. Ithaca, NY: Cornell University Press, 1982.

Maisonnat, Claude. "The Returns of the Reader in *An Outcast of the Islands*." *Yearbook of Conrad Studies* 3 (2007): 67–79.

Moses, Michael Valdez. *The Novel and the Globalization of Culture*. Oxford: Oxford University Press, 1995.

Najder, Zdzisław. *Conrad in Perspective: Essays on Art and Fidelity*. Cambridge: Cambridge University Press, 1997.

– *Joseph Conrad: A Life*. Translated by Halina Najder. New York: Camden House, 2007.

Nicolson, Nigel and Joanne Trautmann, eds. *The Letters of Virginia Woolf*. Volume 2. New York: Harcourt Brace Jovanovich, 1977.

Nietzsche, Friedrich. *The Birth of Tragedy and the Case of Wagner*. Translated by Walter Kaufmann. New York: Vintage Books, 1967.

– "On Ethics." In *The Portable Nietzsche*. Translated by Walter Kaufmann, 30–2. London: Viking Penguin, 1982.

– *Thus Spake Zarathustra: A Book for Everyone and Nobody*. Translated by Graham Parkes. Oxford: Oxford University Press, 2008.

Nussbaum, "Equity and Mercy." In *Sex and Social Justice*. 154–83. Oxford: Oxford University Press, 1999.

– *The Fragility of Goodness: Luck and Ethics in Greek Tragedy and Philosophy*. Cambridge. Cambridge University Press, 1986.

Orr, Leonard. "*Almayer's Folly* (1895) and *An Outcast of the Islands* (1896)." In *A Joseph Conrad Companion*. 27–48. Edited by Leonard Orr and Theodore Billy. Westport, CT: Greenwood Press, 1999.

Paccaud-Huguet, Josiane. "'One of those trifles that awaken ideas': The Conradian Moment." *The Conradian: Journal of the Joseph Conrad Society (UK)* 31, no. 1 (Spring 2006): 75–88.

Panagopoulos, Nic. "Conrad's Poetics: An Aristotelian Reading of *Heart of Darkness*." *L'époque Conradienne* 40 (2015–17): 117–49.

– *The Fiction of Joseph Conrad: The Influence of Schopenhauer and Nietzsche*. London: Peter Lang, 1998.

– "Jim 'Under a Cloud': The Career of a Leitmotif." *Yearbook of Conrad Studies (Poland)*. 12 (2017): 59–69.

– "The Ship of State and Its Captain in Plato and Conrad." *The Conradian: Journal of the Joseph Conrad Society (UK)* 45, no. 1 (Spring 2020): 73–90.

Pfau, Thomas. *Minding the Modern: Human Agency, Intellectual Traditions, and Responsible Knowledge*. Indiana: University of Notre Dame Press, 2013.

Phillips-Garret, Clarissa. *"Sungnōmē* in Aristotle." *Apeiron* 50 no. 3 (2017): 311–33.

Poster, Carol. "Whose Aristotle? Which Aristotelianism? A Historical Prolegomenon to Thomas Farrell's Norms of Rhetorical Culture." *Philosophy and Rhetoric* 41, no. 4 (2008): 375–97.

Proust, Marcel. *Remembrance of Things Past.* Three Volumes. Translated by C.K. Scott Moncrieff and Terence Kilmartin. New York: Random House, 1981.

Ray, Martin. Introduction. *Chance: A Tale in Two Parts,* vii–xix. Oxford: Oxford University Press, 1988.

Roochnik, David. "Teleology as death wish: a Nietzschean critique of Aristotle." 7 February 2014. St. John's College. Annapolis, MD. mp3, 59:07. https://digitalarchives.sjc.edu/items/show/52.

Russell, Bertrand. *Portraits from Memory and Other Essays.* London: George Allen & Unwin, 1956.

Said, Edward. "Conrad and Nietzsche." In *Joseph Conrad: A Commemoration.* 65–76. Edited by Norman Sherry. London: Palgrave Macmillan, 1976.

Salkever, Steven. *Finding the Mean: Theory and Practice in Aristotelian Political Philosophy.* Princeton: Princeton University Press, 1990.

Sewlall, Harry. "Cannibalism in the Colonial Imaginary: A Reading of Joseph Conrad's 'Falk,'" *Journal of Literary Studies* (June 2006): 158–74.

Shakespeare, William. *Hamlet.* Oxford: Oxford University Press, 2008.

Simmons, Allan H. "Conrad, My Conrad. But which *is* my Conrad?" *The Conradian: Journal of the Joseph Conrad Society (U.K.)* 45, no. 1 (Spring 2020): 57–71.

– *Joseph Conrad.* New York: Palgrave Macmillan, 2006.

Sinclair, T.A. Translator's Introduction. *Politics,* edited by Trevor J. Saunders, 13–28. London: Penguin, 1992.

Stape, J.H. Introduction. *An Outcast of the Islands,* ix–xxv. Oxford: Oxford World's Classics, 1992.

Tanner, Tony. "'Gnawed Bones' and 'Artless Tales': Eating and Narrative in 'Falk.'" In *Joseph Conrad: A Commemoration,* edited by Norman Sherry, 17–36. London: Palgrave Macmillan, 1976.

Tessitore, Aristide. *Reading Aristotle's Ethics: Virtue, Rhetoric and Political Philosophy.* Albany: SUNY Press, 1996.

Thorburn, David. *Conrad's Romanticism.* New Haven: Yale University Press, 1974.

Tutein, David. *Conrad's Reading: An Annotated Bibliography.* St. Louis: Locus Hill Press, 1990.

Vlitos, Paul. "Conrad's Ideas of Gastronomy: Dining in 'Falk.'" *Victorian Literature and Culture* 36 (2008): 433–49.

Wall, Steven. "Perfectionism in Moral and Political Philosophy." In *The Stanford Encyclopedia of Philosophy.* Edited by Edward N. Zalta (Fall 2008). http://plato.stanford.edu/archives/fall2008/entries/perfectionism-moral/.

Watt, Ian. *Conrad in the Nineteenth Century*. Berkeley: University of California Press, 1978.

Watts, Cedric. "Thematic Precipitation in Joseph Conrad's Works." *The Conradian: Journal of the Joseph Conrad Society (UK)* 45, no. 2 (Autumn 2020): 65–70.

White, Andrea. "Conrad and Modernism." In *A Historical Guide to Joseph Conrad*, edited by John Peters, 163–96. Oxford: Oxford University Press, 2010.

Woleński, Jan. "The Reception of Aristotle in Poland around 1900." In *Aristote au XIX Siècle*, edited by Denis Thouard, 395–408. Paris: Les Presses Universitaire, Septentrion, 2004.

Wollaeger, Mark A. *Joseph Conrad and the Fictions of Skepticism*. Palo Alto, CA: Stanford University Press, 1990.

Woolf, Virginia. *The Letters of Virginia Woolf, Volume 2*. Edited by Nigel Nicolson and Joanne Trautmann. New York: Harcourt Brace Jovanovich, 1977.

Index

abstraction(s): dehumanizing extremes and, 13; Marlow turning away from, 63; rationality and, 95; theory and, 93, 95

Acheraïou, Amar, rethinking post-colonialism, 6

action: admitting responsibility for, 88; anything incapable of, 106n7; Aristotle on, 21; concept of, 17; Conrad's emphasis on, 22, 112n47; Conrad's focus on intention and, 15, 111n22; Conrad's reference to, 15; consequential outlook on, 88; fullest recognition to world of, 18; importance of, in Conrad's vision, 102–3; limits of, 34; as matter of principle, 90; purposeful, 21; tragic, 21; virtuous, and character, 127n18; word, 19

action [...] nothing but action, Conrad, 17–19, 24, 102

Adams, David, *Colonial Odysseys*, 6

aesthetic unity, 21, 22

Agamben, Giorgio, biopower, 129n61

Agathon (poet), 4, 34

Á la recherche du temps perdus (Proust), 19

Almayer's Folly (Conrad), 10, 26, 32

anagnorisis, recognition, 27, 36–8, 116n55

ancient tragedy: Aristotle's *Poetics*, 59; Conrad's *An Outcast of the Islands*, 7, 8, 15, 24, 25–8, 70, 84; Patusan in *Lord Jim* and, 55–60

Anderson, Walter E., absence of guilt, 79

Annas, Julia, Aristotelian habituation, 97–8

Apollo's temple, "Know thyself!," 37

Aristotle, 4, 5, 6; action, 21; capacity for deliberation, 91; character and experience, 97; concept of discernment, 70; Conrad and, 5–6, 8, 12–13, 19–24, 103; courage, 58; definition of tragedy, 21; doctrine of the mean, 64, 65, 91; *doxa*, 79, 124n55; ethical action, 89; familial relationships in tragic poetry, 52–3; fear and inaction, 50; friendship (*philia*), 77; function of logos or speech, 92; habituation and character-forming, 97–8; hamartia, 27, 46; hero's transition from ignorance to knowledge, 37; human species, 69; inflexible theory, 92, 128n50; naturalistic politics, 124n48–9; nature and,

Ingram Content Group UK Ltd.
Milton Keynes UK
UKHW041813210323
418919UK00016B/228/J